Nicki Jackowska is a gifted novelist, poet and creative writing tutor who has worked with individuals and groups for twenty-five years in various settings and at all levels of experience. Many of her students are widely published, have gained creative writing qualifications and/or have experienced profound changes in themselves and their lives.

Author of nine books and winner of numerous awards including an Arts Council Bursary for fiction, Nicki is also a supremely talented performer and speaker. As well as giving solo readings, she works with Irish musicians and continues to explore the interaction of words with music, dance and the visual arts, as tutor and participant, in both workshop and performance.

Lighting a Slow Fuse – Selected Poems will be published by Enitharmon in 1998. Her lifelong interest in analytical psychology combined with ongoing explorations of art and language, form the basis of her new book on Jung and lost worlds. She is also working on a novel, *The Lost Gardens of Mariamne*, and her sixth poetry collection, *Spikenard*.

WRITE FOR LIFE

How to Inspire Your Creative Writing

Nicki Jackowska

ELEMENT

Shaftesbury, Dorset ● Rockport, Massachusetts
Melbourne, Victoria

© Element Books 1997
Text © Nicki Jackowska 1997

First published in Great Britain in 1997 by
Element Books Limited
Shaftesbury, Dorset SP7 8BP

Published in the USA in 1997 by
Element Books, Inc.
PO Box 830, Rockport, MA 01966

Published in Australia in 1997 by
Element Books
and distributed by Penguin Australia Ltd
487 Maroondah Highway, Ringwood, Victoria 3134

Cover design by Mark Slader
Page design by Roger Lightfoot
Typeset by Bournemouth Colour Press
Printed and bound in Great Britain by
J. W. Arrowsmith, Bristol

British Library Cataloguing in Publication
data available

Library of Congress Cataloging in Publication
data available

ISBN 1–86204–148–2

CONTENTS

PART II   EXPANSIONS

PART III   FROM ONE TO ANOTHER

PART IV   SAMPLES

FOR LAURA

who helped to keep our house
An Chy Kerensa

Gratitude to all my friends, colleagues and students for their support, contributions and clarification of ideas during the writing of this book.

For particular help in the last weeks of writing, love and thanks to my sister Carol.

ACKNOWLEDGEMENTS

The author and the publishers would like to thank the following for permission to reproduce copyright material:

Lines 38–40 from the poem 'The Circus Animals' Desertion' and lines 157–8 from the poem 'Meditations in Time of Civil War' by W. B. Yeats reproduced by permission of A. P. Watt Ltd on behalf of Michael Yeats. Lines from 'The Circus Animals' Desertion' reprinted with the permission of Simon and Schuster from *The Collected Works of W. B. Yeats*, Volume 1: *The Poems*, revised and edited by Richard J. Finneran. Copyright 1940 by Georgie Yeats; copyright renewed © 1968 by Bertha Georgie Yeats, Michael Butler Yeats, and Anne Yeats. Lines from 'Meditations in Time of Civil War' reprinted with the permission of Simon and Schuster from *The Collected Works of W. B. Yeats*, Volume 1: *The Poems*, revised and edited by Richard J. Finneran. Copyright 1928 by Macmillan Publishing Company; copyright renewed © 1956 by Georgie Yeats;

Margaret Snow and the W. S. Graham Estate for permission to use the extract from the poem 'The Secret Name' by W. S. Graham, published in his collection *Implements in Their Places* (Faber and Faber, 1977);

The Nicholas Treadwell Gallery, London for permission to reproduce 'The First Horseman of the Apocalypse' by Malcolm Poynter (sculpture in rubbish/paper pulp/resin, 1980–2).

The extract from Tony Harrison's 'Timer', published in his *Selected Poems* (King Penguin) appears by kind permission of the poet, c/o Gordon Dickerson.

The extract from Craig Raine's poem 'In the Mortuary', published in his collection *A Martian Sends a Postcard Home* (Oxford University Press, 1979) appears by permission of Oxford University Press.

Every effort has been made to trace all copyright holders, but if any have been inadvertently overlooked the author and publishers will be pleased to make the necessary arrangement at the first opportunity.

FOREWORD

When I began writing, there were few formal organizations for the sharing of work, for guidance or response. I was brought up in a non-artistic household and it has always been a puzzle to me how I came to have such a passion for language, painting, theatre. Perhaps emotional expression, if blocked, has to find other routes into the light. This is one explanation.

In my own life, I believe more than one factor to have been the cause. Had I not moved to Cornwall in my teens, and then again in 1968 when I stayed for six years and not just twelve months; had I not, prior to that, engaged in the emotional work of acting and all its self-shaping; had I not been swept into the explosion of blues and folk music before and after my six years in the theatre; had I not met and married a visual artist – then I might never have made writing, performing and tutoring my life's work. All these factors, and many more, are woven together into a thick rope. Even now I can trace a single thread – gold or black as it may be – a long way back.

The landscape of West Penwith, Cornwall, is harsh and challenging, the quality of its light transparent and also a fierce gold. The land itself both invites and repels. It seems I have breathed these things in almost through the pores of my skin, along with the writers, musicians and artists I met there. Also farmers, potters, fishermen, people working raw material.

I have always been drawn to contrasts and contradictions – a marriage of opposites. Needing to explore on a more intellectual level, I took a degree in Philosophy at the University of Sussex as a mature student, after the birth of my daughter Laura. The rigours of such a degree had both positive and negative affects. Again, the emotional and imaginative world, not able to emerge in the academic work, went underground or took a side seat, but gave rise to my novel – that quirky and outrageous play of opposites, *Doctor Marbles and Marianne – A Romance*. This was my first published fiction.

Writing can be born and reborn, as we ourselves are. My

novel was born as an alternative to the particular disciplines of the degree. Something was born in me in Cornwall and my meetings there with other writers. This became my first collection of poetry, *The House That Manda Built*. And now, for example, a chance meeting with an old friend in Wales, an overgrown garden on the Hafod Estate, the haunting quality of a name (Mariamne) have together become the bedrock of the novel I'm now working on.

I think of myself as an archaeologist, excavating the depths and possibilities of the human psyche, the work of imagination. I think of the journey of my life as a spiral. It may be necessary to return to the same place many times, whether that 'place' is an event in memory, a place in landscape, a few potent words held in my notebook. Each time, I draw something new up from the moment, gather my experiences to sense and express more closely the heart of the matter.

What is certain is that none of this is easy. Even now, after all these years living and writing in cities, villages, isolated dwellings, I must face the same challenges, am plagued by the same questions. For example, to take a journey or remain at my desk, to go where the impulse takes me or to stick with a master-plan. How to manage a balance of heart and hand – we all face this, whatever our work. It is no different for a writer.

I bring to my students not method, but the possibility of a method for them. One cannot write with total randomness for any length of time without feeling lost or adrift, nor follow a tightly structured course without some sacrifice of one's individuality. As a tutor, I would say that my primary approach has always been a readiness to meet students in the place where they are. This can involve engagement with the events of their lives both past and present, their environment and relationships, the way they see things. I look for the place of discontent, sometimes of breakage. If we are starting from scratch, I will have many beginnings to offer, but which is chosen will always depend on the circumstances – one-to-one tutorial, size of workshop group, the length of time we are to work together, students' prior experience. If we are not starting from scratch, then my input will be different.

I will engage with what has been written, ease or tease it forward, provide new angles and perspectives. Since I have worked in classrooms, marquees, corridors, fields, terraces, at firesides; at dawn and midnight; with the same student or students for one hour, one day, one week, or several years; in all weathers and seasons; in cities or remote and ancient houses, then the capturing of a formula here is not only undesirable, but impossible. Since I suggest nothing to students that I have not myself undertaken (though we travel differently and end up in different places), you can be sure that these pages have the authority of being rooted in my own life-experience.

The particular final form of work cannot be known in advance. When I am working with a student on that final fine-tuning, we are beyond theory, though we may have picked up, held or discarded a number of theories along the way. The poem or story's own life and form will itself provide the answers as to what's to be done. Where the balance lies, whether it may need an unexpected twist in a new direction, right at the last. This can involve a subtle and intricate interaction between a student and myself, informed by our previous time together. A quicksilver activity, too fine to catch. I prefer to avoid postal tutoring which leaves out this most valuable presence with all that it makes possible, its multi-layered interactions. I can guide, surprise, wrestle, turn the writing this way and that from beginning to end of the process. But I cannot give you a formula, or something called a 'right way'.

In this sense, creative writing cannot be taught. If it could, you would write in my shadow; or in abstraction.

I am interested in the work of midwifery, or fellow-travelling. Your writing will emerge in its own light.

If you are coming to creative writing for the first time, you may feel the need for directions. This book has been written in a way that makes possible many kinds of use, offering source material which can be moulded, sifted or arranged in sequence according to your needs. Or used almost randomly, into which you can dip and pull out a theme or direction.

All these methods – or non-methods! – are part of a writer's life. When setting out, however, too many choices can be overwhelming, so here are suggestions to help you locate yourself and make good use of this book as you begin:

- Provide yourself with a special journal which will be your valued space for all the various kinds of writing you will do. This will be your own storehouse and place of exploration.
- Choose a place in your house which has a particular feeling for you, somewhere to 'go to' when you write. If this room, desk, table, corner, bed, mat can also accommodate small objects, so much the better.
- If possible, choose a particular time of day for your writing. This will depend on your domestic circumstances and can be changed or extended as you become more sure of yourself. This disciplined decision-making is essential for establishing a sense of purpose and value from the beginning.
- Time your sessions. Establishing firm boundaries and sticking to them is generative in itself. An hour each day would be ideal. If this can't be managed, then less. But decide on a length of time you can rely on and maintain, stick to it, and use a clock or watch to begin and end your writing time.
- To read the entire book and *then* begin may be overwhelming. I have deliberately arranged the chapters so that ideas are always supported by practical suggestions, and every section has its accompanying writing activity. Take one chapter for each day's writing time. Read it first, choose *one* suggested writing practice and stay with that.
- When you have worked through a number of chapters and begin to feel the need to go over what you have written, decide that next day's writing time will be devoted to 'review'.
  Suggested time-spans for this:
  - Six consecutive days, one chapter each day with Day Seven for reading over and deciding which day's work has been most important for you.
  - A number of weeks following this pattern, either continuing with new chapters, or staying with the first six chapters but a new writing idea.
  - One week trying out new beginnings each day and one week for development. Continue to alternate these.

The important point is to make decisions in advance. When your journal feels a trusted place over which you have some control, when you feel a close relationship with your journal and the activity of writing, then is the time to improvise, change direction, use the book in more varied ways.

In addition to locating a specific place and time for writing, keep your journal with you whenever you can. As time goes on, you will find yourself jotting down words and phrases more frequently, as your writing extends and language begins to take its place in your life in this new way.

INTRODUCTION

On 14 February 1989, the *fatwa* or death sentence was pronounced on the writer Salman Rushdie for the alleged blasphemy to Islam in his novel *The Satanic Verses*. This *fatwa* was issued by the leader of the Muslim world at that time, the Ayatollah Khomeini. Even though the Ayatollah has since died, the death sentence on Rushdie has never been revoked, and a narrow section of the Muslim people would wish it to be carried out.

On 14 February 1992, a number of writers wrote speeches about the implications of this and gathered together at a public meeting in London to share views and express their support for Rushdie.

There was something of the vital importance (*vita* = life, vital = of life) of writing in Gunter Grass's presentation, as also in his insistence that a threat upon Salman Rushdie is a threat to us all. Thus Grass took the argument beyond questions of what is being said in a man's writing – whether it be blasphemous or no – and touched upon the issue of the death that can occur when the capacity to write is stoppered (or even denied) and writing itself is suppressed or dies for lack of use. Without the dimensions opened up *in us* by writing, parts of us – dimensions or possibilities of us – die.

Gunter Grass's point was, of course, essential to Salman Rushdie's situation and all the issues this gives rise to. But for me he introduced that most important question of what it means, and what are the means, to be fully alive as a human being. And how the existence and practice of writing itself, for everyone and anyone, is that which makes us human in its capacity to hold the world open; to hold open choice, ambiguity and that most important of attributes – to see and know the world in many different ways.

We do not need to define ourselves as writers for this to be true. Some people write to earn a living from it. Others write to explore, with no further issue or outcome than that of personal discovery. And between these two polarities lies a whole spectrum of activity from those who publish in small ways or locally to those who publish with major imprints yet earn their basic living from some other work altogether.

There is common ground between those who put pen to paper and receive money for it and those who don't, whether the results are publishable or not. When we write, we embark upon a process which has more implications, effects and results than are at first apparent.

Writing might be thought of in terms such as these: that we are *merely* thinking aloud, *merely* recording a moment so that it isn't forgotten; off-loading an intense and perhaps unmanageable emotion or emotions on to the page. We may be doing all of these things, but the word or idea I would question here is 'merely'. This word dismisses, devalues and distorts what we are doing when we write and also provides an effective blockage to what is going on.

It is my aim in this book to remove that blockage, dismantle the many assumptions which have often become fixed edifices concerning the writing act. I dig down underneath the notion (or smoke-screen) that language is a tool or currency of mainly utilitarian value, a measurable substance of barter and exchange, and attempt to reveal its true potential as an unquantifiable and complex movement by which our world is shaped, seen and thought about; the means by which we ourselves become what we are.

And so I hope to open up a veritable Pandora's Box – or uncover a nest of vipers – whichever you prefer.

I suspect it might be both.

There will be nothing here that I have not lived through for myself. In the course of 25 years of work I have created, or stumbled upon, many roles for the writer and come to see the practice of writing as everything from off-load to nothing less than the expansion of the world and myself at one and the same time; the writer as director, actor, fly-on-the-wall, camera, dancer, juggler. Alternately master and slave. Located in cellar or attic. In disguise or painfully, rawly exposed. Witness, cheat, fool, magpie, joker, burglar.

Writing multiplies, makes many. Makes manifest. It calls up many worlds and so gives back to the wielder of the pen (and his audience of readers) a multitude of roles, moods, gratifications, invitations and perhaps testing grounds. It is also powerful enough to create another space and time altogether, a 'fictional space' which enters our own or into which we enter, even when writing a letter.

I will use my own life-journey as a faithful and also treacherous storehouse of the mean, the intransigent, the unique particular and the sacred. Whatever is or is not permitted by Islam, by Christianity or by a world shrinking into uniformity, however much this seems belied by the proliferation of a variety of nations and a variety of 'entertainments' – the use and practice of imagination, invention, realization *for oneself* by way of the written word or speech, can have no censors.

And if the censors do nag and spit out of some childhood arena, or rap on the spirit with intent to kill, then they too may be called to task. By banishment or perhaps more subtle trickery. Coaxing them to listen, perhaps. The father who panicked and struck his blows at your blossoming may, in retrospect, creep a little closer to the blaze. The mother who oiled the wheels for you a mite too well, turns not a hair as your sexuality blasts across the page like a lightning conductor.

March 6th, Michelangelo was born. God giving life to Adam. We can all enter into the mind of a creator and ignite each other.

And in case this is too cosmic, too spiritual a realm, we can come closer to earth and a gentler, less apocalyptic handing-on of the means of waking into life.

'If you will bear with me a minute' is what I often hear when making a phone enquiry to the bank, British Rail, whatever. It seems to be the current phrase to soothe consumers. Let me use it too, for this book (which cannot help but be partial and selective), for it asks for attention, acceptance and patience. And however many manuscripts are hand-shredded and however many writing-days die in a tidal wave of wine, yet in the end we are forced to attend, to see what our writing is becoming and what is coming into the light.

Or take the short paragraph on the cover of Michael Ondaatje's novel, *In the Skin of a Lion*: 'The first sentence of every novel should be: "Trust me, this will take time but there is order here, very faint, very human."' Say that to the censors but above all say it to yourself – the censor almost indistinguishable from you. And perhaps it is possible to hear this invitation sent back and forth between the world we inhabit, the shifting world of our restless imaginations, and the page itself, glaring at us like a huge eye and daring us to enter and begin.

If you read this book from the beginning, you will first of all be presented with a number of ideas. These ideas will be spelled out in a series of short sections or mini-chapters. They will explore what writing and the use of language can do. They will also show both how writing changes your mind and how changing your mind can make writing happen. Also how important writing can be in experimenting with and proving a changed mind. You will see how writing can change the world; how for simplicity's sake I'll talk of three active protagonists in the writing and changing process: *yourself* (your mind and imagination); *the world* (your room, town, country, the planet – a series of interlocking environments moving at different speeds); *the words on the page* (from one to infinity, alone or in collaboration).

If you read this book from the beginning, the first section will give rise to openings, shifts, disturbances and questions. In which case you will not begin the suggested writing practices which follow 'as you are', but will perhaps have already moved a little out of yourself. You will have extended the possibility of this practice before you begin.

I'm calling this opening section 'a basket of currencies', a term so irritatingly applied to the money markets which are spoken of as though they are autonomous, self-propelling beings carrying us along behind. I shall discuss writing as a way of resisting the many ways in which we are taught, cajoled, persuaded, bullied or brainwashed into being 'carried along behind' and how through writing and its associative processes we can regain a little more of ourselves. Claim back those parts which have never been uncovered and provoked into life. Or that we have unwittingly allowed to be stolen, denied or stifled. Writing will be many things, but primarily it will be challenge on all fronts. Together with nourishment for our selves and others.

We can see this basket of currencies in terms of a grid of energies with currents moving in all directions. Each of the 18 sections can be used as a thought for each single day for almost three weeks, together with one or more of the suggestions for writing. Or lengthen the time-scale, with one chapter each week. You may find that a particular chapter/idea takes hold more strongly, and you would like to work with the idea until it runs out of steam. You may want to read the book in the usual manner from beginning to end, and *then* map out a plan for its use for you. To revisit and cross-fertilize the sections in a way that best feeds your own activity.

I believe in a mixture of thought and practice – mixture meaning things that are bound together. The opening sections are not a 'body of theory' or an 'analysis of' the writing process and so abstracted from it. I hope you will find that the ideas and exercises constantly interweave. And that if you were to ignore the opening thoughts and begin with the assorted assignments, practices, channels and directions of Part IV, none the less the ideas I've presented would emerge of themselves out of the activity. The list of aims, ideas and practices in Part IV does not follow any particular order as explored in the book but tells you what you can expect to *emerge* through idea and practice throughout your investigations. For example, the word 'disabled' as applied to a person is an idea I particularly dislike in that it suggests a fixed category of human being. It also implies that to be 'disabled' is to be less-than-perfect, and that other people who are not disabled are somehow whole and superior. This idea has had appalling outcomes where the myth of a superior or master-race has taken hold of an entire nation and has been applied to its extremity by political means. A word can catch hold and lodge in the minds of whole nations and become the trigger-force for anything from baiting to mass extinction.

Although 'the disabled' are a group defined as such by society and by those who care for them, if we take the word away from its prime meaning as applying to an entire person or categorizing them entirely and think of it in a far more fluid and partial way as applying to this or that process as being temporarily curtailed, then the word takes on a whole new dimension.

'Disabled' is therefore a condition that every human being will have to encounter for themselves at some time or another, as a temporary or long-term *lack of ability*, in this or that context, physical or psychological.

I have a temporary disability. I can't use a knife with my left hand since I've cut my thumb. Or I can't 'face' that person today, she's too disturbing. I won't keep the appointment. I am 'not able' to meet her.

Two things at once become apparent: that words have unbridled power to shape or determine our perception of others and ourselves, unless we *intervene* and re-use language to our purpose. Which means of course that we then need to find out what our purpose is. Also that generalized categories often produce a kind of 'blanket constriction', pinning the subject within that category; a form of imprisonment. As soon as we question and unravel what lies within such generalizations, we produce *particular* examples, make *comparisons*, *suppose* the situation were like this. Then we unlock and permit to have its play the saving, redeeming power of language in its quality of discrimination, exactitude and compassionate sifting of elements into a broader and more generous conjuring.

In the course of working with myself and students I have found that certain ideas and perceptions arise again and again, sometimes springing into the space from nowhere like a jack-in-the-box and taking you by surprise. Sometimes recognized from a long way off, approaching slowly and demanding attention for many days together. Like a stranger introducing himself warily but stepping firmly across the threshold. So that if you read Part III in relation to specific groups of people with whom you don't identify and find that something I've suggested opens doors for you, don't be surprised. We are complex creatures with many hidden corners. We can find aspects of ourselves which will enable us to identify with a wider range of people than we'd realized we could. In this our possibilities for discovery and relationship are virtually unlimited. We can resist the implicit and explicit denial of these possibilities which assaults us from many quarters. Our culture and its leaders, political and otherwise, do not promote our individuality, its expression in words. Its relationships.

PART I

A Basket of Currencies

'Who are *you*?' said the Caterpillar.

This was not an encouraging opening for a conversation. Alice replied, rather shyly, 'I – I hardly know, sir, just at present – at least I know who I *was* when I got up this morning, but I think I must have been changed several times since then.'

Lewis Carroll, *Alice's Adventures in Wonderland*

'*Must* a name mean something?' Alice asked doubtfully.

'Of course it must,' Humpty Dumpty said with a short laugh: '*my* name means the shape I am – and a good handsome shape it is, too. With a name like yours you might be any shape, almost.'

'When *I* use a word,' Humpty Dumpty said in a rather scornful tone, 'it means just what I choose it to mean – neither more nor less.'

'The question is,' said Alice, 'whether you *can* make words mean different things.'

'The question is,' said Humpty Dumpty, 'which is to be master – that's all.'

'That's a great deal to make a word mean,' Alice said in a thoughtful tone.

'When I make a word do a lot of work like that,' said Humpty Dumpty, 'I always pay it extra.'

Lewis Carroll, *Through the Looking Glass*

PROLOGUE

If you think of this book as a landscape crossed with many paths, forks, bends and corners, you'll be the better equipped to use it fully. Ideas, themes and images will emerge and re-emerge in different forms and by various channels. And differently coloured according to the context and the point of view. So that we are, as it were, turning an idea in our hands like a multi-faceted crystal. Or looking at a number of shots of the same thing taken in different weathers with different lenses in the camera. Close-up or long-shot, and so on, through the viewfinder.

Primarily we may write for ourselves, to create an external space on which to project and invent ourselves. And at the same time we may be writing for a nameless sea of human beings, without particular identity. Then again, we may write in opposition to or in relation to a particular person who has great significance in our lives.

It doesn't matter. What matters is that to write is to create a place external to ourselves that is separate and distinct and in which we may know ourselves and each other better. We are, necessarily, engaging in *public activity*, and here lies the foundation for that creation, now separate, to go further.

On out into the world.

And to take effect.

And to interfere.

1 THE MOMENT OF IGNITION

It is often the case that a barrier to writing may lie in the assumption that the starting-point for writing *must* come from a single, particular attitude, frame of mind or 'thing'. Writing often begins from the spark created when two or more things collide or interact. A line from Wallace Stevens given as a workshop theme: 'In the corner an old sailor is dreaming of tigers in red weather' (*Tiger*). When a connection is made with a childhood memory of imaginary wild animals lurking under the stair, then does the poem begin to move. Or, in one of my own poems, the fragments of Simone's outfit as she dances: 'a quick twist of silver' contrasts with the scarred face of her partner, yet 'ignites' the poem (*Simone Dances*).

The myths are many and I'd suggest that they are wily and cunning in their hold on us. This gathering of myths may be seen as an octopus: when you chop off one tentacle, there are a dozen more waiting to enfold you. We can be substantially enclosed by an idea just as surely as we can be locked within prison walls.

Ideas and word-practice will jostle, intermingle and cross-fertilize within these pages so that it can be seen that they are entirely dependent upon each other if there is to be growth and advancement.

I'm looking at ideas in two ways here.

Firstly, there are ideas *about* writing: the idea that I've already presented – that we can be prevented from writing by an octopus-like manipulation of all kinds of images and prejudices about what starts us off.

Then there is the suggestion that we can 'be started'. The ignition key can be turned by any number of factors, including ideas, and sometimes a collision or conjunction of apparently unrelated happenings, whether 'idea' or 'thing'.

I was watching a television programme recently in which the biologist Miriam Rothschild was explaining how her wild-flower seeds came up randomly. Even though there was the same number of seeds for each flower in the packet, there was always a concentration of either poppy, cornflower, corncockle. As she talked, I was thinking about the *idea* of randomness, but I also had a strong internal image of my father, knobbly-kneed, pushing through a field in his old battered hat. My father popped up, as it were, in the middle of a clump of wild flowers. And I remembered I'd once likened his eyes to the blue of cornflowers in a poem, way back. The external image of a process in nature (in this case on television), linked with an internal image or memory, creates a spark caused by the juxtaposition of outer and inner worlds.

Such moments can be our ignition and looking out for these is part of the process. An act of vigilance, a state of preparedness to catch the connection.

Like a butterfly-catcher, we can think of netting-in things in flight, ideas and images on the wing. This is one way of looking at it. But we can be more active and intervene. Hunting for ignition-points is itself part of the enterprise. There is no one correct way to generate the interest that will kick-start us into our life-on-the-page.

The idea that you must be in 'a-creative-frame-of-mind' (whatever that is), or the idea that to sit in solitude in a beautiful 'poetic' setting without fear of interruption will guarantee a flow of words, are equally suspect.

The work or practice can take place in a very different way. It may be that the *idea* will create the spark – ie something conjured in the mind without reference to specific present material objects, events, etc. For example, I can say 'Love is always accompanied by a feeling of loss', and this idea can come to me in a state of rêverie, that drifting, in-between condition almost like dreaming when awake. The movement that follows will then be from the abstract to the concrete. You will need to find images for your idea to live in or the result will be empty generalizations and the feeling that this has been said a hundred times before and, what's more, said *exactly like this*. Images of loss may be broken things: eggshells, cups. Or signs of departure – a knotted hand, broken wing, one upturned shoe. The writing grounds the idea in these concrete things.

Or we can start at the opposite end of the process with words themselves; playing with words on a page, the performing of an exercise for its own sake, perhaps with a blind faith in this activity *of itself* creating the opening or openings for our word-hoard or narrative. It may be that you will try an exercise several times to no effect and then suddenly, as though out of nowhere, the connection is made. Reverse the process above and begin with a broken eggshell and what then comes to mind.

To use an example from another area of exchange; you may have been talking to a friend in a direct and conscious way about a recent distressing experience when, for example, you lost your temper and threw a precious object and it shattered. You can try simply describing the sequence of events, what happened. The experience memorized and recalled with something of its emotional charge *activated* by the telling.

Now imagine another situation and another kind of exchange altogether. Without any specific purpose, I was working with a close friend and Seiki-Jutsu healer, Malcolm Ritchie. I was lying on an exercise mat and Malcolm was shaking my legs about in a floppy manner, rather carelessly I thought. Suddenly, without warning, it felt *unkind* – malignant almost. Without being prepared for it, I was suddenly furiously angry. I was transported to another place, a kitchen, an old kitchen, a bird was trapped. My hand clenched round an old vase and I lifted it and thrust it out into the space and its splinters cascaded across a stone floor.

I am talking about what an arbitrary activity of the body can call up or conjure. Emotion and scenario here erupted together, presented themselves uninvited and unlooked-for.

In the first example, you began with the intention of telling a particular story which you already had in mind. In the second example, I was plunged into another reality without intention or motive.

Our stories can begin anywhere. To realize this is to open up the potential for writing, for expression, from many dimensions. One can say that a trigger of whatever kind can release or unleash a swarm (hornet's nest) of associations.

We are the caretakers of vast areas of experience and activity, both our own and also that which we may invent. And which will be 'charged' with 'our own' in the sense of connection or emotional or atmospheric mood.

You may have to tolerate an amount of boredom and repetition, approaching again and again the particular given task. Suddenly it will fire up, or unfold. And reveal perhaps that there has been work going on and movement all along. Hidden work and movement that at a certain point will surface and reveal itself. Whether by means of a natural development or sheer doggedness or a particular pattern of conscious or directed 'poking about'.

Writing can emerge from virtually any corner of ourselves, whether we define 'self' as body, mind, consciousness, memory, imagination. Or from any aspect of the world around us – near or distant, past or present.

Or from any landscape we care to invent.

Practice

A fundamental aim in all writing should be what I call *beating the cliché*.

1) Conjuring – the body.

Decide on situations which use your body differently than normally. Try to catch whatever images occur if you:
a) Walk tall as though you have suddenly grown.
b) Throw stones into the woods/sea aggressively.

Try to 'catch' whatever drifts through you – faces, fragments, objects, rooms. What glimmers out of past or future.

Write them down.

2) Conjuring – emotions.

Write a list of strong emotion-words: RAGE, LUST, ENVY, JEALOUSY, JOY, FEAR, LOVE.

Decide upon a length of time and use a watch.

Feed each word to yourself in turn.

Write quickly and without censoring yourself, whatever things, events, people, fragments are called up by that word. Don't use another word which means the same thing, e.g. FEAR – TERROR. Loosen your mind. Don't worry about grammar, the bizarre, the ridiculous.

Write detail, specifically.

Such as: FEAR – wire, fence, narrow mesh, chicken-peck, blood-spurt, nail going in. Like a nail.

3) Conjuring – memory-association.

Choose a number of objects, imagined or picked out from your environment.

If objects present with you, focus on each one.

If imagined, write its name to make a list.

Again, take each one in turn and time your focus on it.

Write whatever comes to mind and try to paint vivid pictures.

Such as: KEY – door, broken splintering wood, frill of rust, keyhole world. Slit, hand showing, slice of face. Melon-face.

Useful reminders to get you going:
a) What does it look like?
b) What does it remind me of?
c) What does it make me feel?

Do all these things in different places:
a) On a walk (take a notebook).
b) Inside, then outside.
c) Morning, then evening.
   Try different time-spans: one minute, five minutes.
   Also make notes about what happens.

2 WORDS AND YOU

It is something we don't think about often, if at all – the way we ourselves are shaped by the words we use. Both to refer to ourselves, to other people and to the world in general.

For a start, words can have a confining effect, such as happens when we refer to a woman as 'housewife'. It is a form of dismissal, with its generalization acting as a blurring factor. Using this word is what I call accepting 'ready-made' language, the 'near-at-hand'. We pick the most convenient term and it *stops* us thinking and exploring. And, what's more, experiencing the full extent of a person's quality and individuality.

People can be lulled into a cliché-ridden world whereby they are even more easily manipulated by images and slogans from 'above'.

Now it's clear that we can't all the time stop to replace and undo these reductions of what a person can be. In the practical, utilitarian world we need to use the most convenient, easily accepted term of reference – for quick identification, for emergency, for commerce. We are busy, we keep it short.

But this book is dedicated to the idea that if this utilitarian use of words is *all* we do, then the question arises as to what is happening to us. Is this *all* we are for ourselves, we may ask, or for each other? Is this the sum of what the world and/or expression of the world can be? The relationship that is possible between myself and you, between myself and the world I inhabit is curtailed or extended by the attention to and use of words, and conjunctions of words.

To do something about this, I must extend or change my perception. Changing my perception and changing the words I use go hand in hand. In using as my example the word 'housewife', I am in no way devaluing *what we know that word to mean.* It means what it says: a woman who spends all or some of her time working at home and looking after the house she lives in, probably with her husband or partner and their children.

But what if we say: she is a woman who is able to generate her house each day, *as though* (note the phrase) each day were a voyage, who is in intimate contact with walls, linen, china, wood. Who patches and mends and smoothes the rough edges. Who has the power and dignity to shape the day for herself. Who watches how the light changes as sunlight shifts its channel across floor and cloth. In other words, when we probe further into our hackneyed word, we open up a universe of *relationship* that was previously hidden or non-existent.

Whether the woman or man is writing or reading this, whether it applies to him/her or no, it is a world and life different *in kind* that is created by 'housewife' and the longer stretch of words I've used here. Whoever writes or reads has the opportunity to identify with either.

And here's the further potency of language: by using it to delve deeper into our own or another's situation, we can in fact call into being and actually *create* that relationship, where it did not exist before. We allow it to be there. We insist it be there. And so, conversely, we may be using language in such a way that it has the power to create a mood or way of relating *for us*. I decide to write it differently, I force or insist that it is different. The words we use can take us to somewhere we haven't been before.

A friend of mine, the painter Charlotte Jennings, calls this 'the third dimension':

> This third dimension emerges from that twilight zone of the pre-conception where the materials and the hand and the eye make conscious that which would not have been known – that which *could not have been at all* – had it not been for the act of creating it.
>
> Charlotte Jennings, 1991 (my italics)

I'd make one further suggestion here: that there may be more than a third dimension! Since we use words all the time for daily use and do not paint for the same purpose, it is easy to overlook that *using language differently* can be the equivalent to painting in this act of either 'making conscious that which was hidden' or, in a sense, creating that which didn't exist at all beforehand. Either angle on this will do. Or perhaps we can say that these worlds exist as possibilities and it's up to us to bring them into life.

An important reminder here: there is all the difference between the fleeting moment of the 'spoken' and the act of commitment and shaping that is involved in writing it down. When we write it down, we are 'pushing' a material and visible thing, almost like using clay. We can send our sentence this way and that. We can pause and respond to what we have written. We can say, is there more here to find? We can identify our well-worn phrase and stretch further to find something fuller, that adds more contours.

Let me give you another very different example of language-use and how it affects our relationship to things. Many bombs were used in the Second World War. The first two atom bombs were dropped on Hiroshima and Nagasaki. Bombs fell on Vietnam and in the Gulf War. Many of these bombs were given names, sometimes of loved ones. 'Fat Man' and 'Little Boy' were the names given to the atom bombs dropped on Hiroshima and Nagasaki.

Imagine for a moment what happens to the connection we have with these weapons if the word 'nuclear warhead' is replaced by 'Fat Man'. Isn't it the case, as it is with names like Enola Gay, that the death-dealing quality of the weapon is obscured by the familiarity and affection contained in the name of a person or an affectionate nickname? A certain humour and ease are called up. A defusing, you might say, of the bomb's true nature and intention. And if we give the bomb we will drop the name of our own or someone else's girlfriend, isn't it somehow just a family affair or somehow morally more justifiable since our love or defence of our love is somehow contained in the act of slaughter?

Our relationship to the weapon, obscured as it is in this way, is radically altered into a routine, easy-going and somewhat jovial familiarity. The bomb is translated and so is our relationship to it.

To humanize and personalize the inhuman and devastating is language used for the purpose of maintaining or creating a lie. The phraseology of nuclear warfare acts *upon us* as a smoke-screen. We should be aware, therefore, that to accept such naming and to be unaware of its effect, is to collude in our own disempowerment. We are duped, soothed, disarmed by such use. As we are also by such terms as 'collateral damage', which refers to the extinction (genocide) of vast numbers of human beings who are part of the civilian population and not taking up arms.

With such awareness, then, the practice of using language in a way that opposes its use by others to disarm and deceive us and keep us quiet, can be seen as an act of resistance. It is an act of resistance to dismantle and reject a certain use of language, as well as searching out the language of a deeper truth as for celebration, revealing, recovery, the unfolding of new directions for ourselves and the discovery of new areas within.

A positive approach to this would be to seek out such smoke-screens in current programmes or newspapers. To identify words which distort or dehumanize and to write our own real or imagined narrative instead. We can accept, for example, any number of newspaper accounts of the murder of a child by children, the most notorious being the murder of James Bulger in Liverpool, England. The children who did this were themselves subjected to abusive language. One could write an abusive letter exploring the limits of one's own darker feeling. Or imagine the thoughts of one of the children as a series of word fragments. No writing can avoid pain, just as we can't. Or begin an account with 'It was *as if* ...', using many imagined routes into the event. Where was the child's father, what was he doing just before it happened? What were the details of his day, before it was broken?

Choosing to tell in many different ways can only release and expand experience and relationship. Prevent the stifling sense of finality that comes when the single word summarizes all, and 'killer' is the be-all and the end of it. Even if it gives us a spurious temporary relief.

Practice

1) Releasing the fullness of experience.

 Make a list of simple domestic actions, taking care to use the most common word for such things.

 Take each one in turn and 'uncover' its full potential.

 Don't resist comparisons and metaphors, eg ironing: the iron sailed across the shirt-sleeve like a liner, the tip digging a furrow in my ... and so forth.

2) Make a list of potentially dangerous objects that could perhaps be used as weapons. Take each in turn. Examples might be knives, scissors – but also more obviously harmless things.

 Write about each in its 'disarming' form, eg shape, texture, that which pleases and doesn't threaten.

Then make it dangerous. Write about it again, activate it dangerously so that you are focusing on another potential aspect of its nature.

(You can use objects that are 'benign' when functioning normally but become 'dangerous' when malfunctioning. I'm thinking of gas ovens, leaks, also escalators in the underground. Use the most vivid words you can. Explore the differences.)

Note how object and relationship change as you approach it *by way of words* in first one way, then another.

3 NOT EITHER/OR BUT BOTH

No one can begin from a vacuum. Some 25 years back, I was fortunate to find myself in an area of England with a concentration of eccentric and accessible writers who were only too willing to share ideas and pass on discoveries. That I learned such things in a social situation was only one way of achieving some kind of apprenticeship. That many things I learned caused profound disturbance and change to my*self* was something I'd not expected.

I discovered that received ideas about time, perspective, perception, memory, history, emotions, reality itself would need to be called into question. I discovered that narrative, fictional or poetic spaces are the illuminators of what we call 'real space' – our own, often dulled, everyday environment. That words and the worlds they evoke are powerful indeed and that no longer could I hold to the belief that writing is an orderly activity, proceeding in a linear fashion from A to B, the serious and studious setting-down of an inspiration or vision – a copying-down of an already existing entity.

As soon as one begins to write, one selects, invents, re-orders. What it is that arises or comes out of the process in the end is always some kind of mix of the already existing and the created or invented.

All this may be hard to swallow, but it is infinitely easier once you stop worrying about it and trying to force what you write to match exactly what you have seen, known or experienced. It's to one's advantage also to stop worrying about the false dichotomy that is set up around that anxious question: yes, but surely it isn't proper literature if it's having a therapeutic affect? Or conversely: this is literature, an objective activity which can't have anything to do with therapy.

I have never been able to understand why some people find it necessary to insist on this division. There are two answers: the fact that an activity *must be* of one kind or another and that we must choose what kind it is to be, forms part of a philosophical and materialist tradition (and perhaps also Newtonian physics!) that is unable to grasp or take on board the idea of dialectic, ambiguity, multiple perspective and multi-dimensional reality.

The man or woman who writes is a complex creature. He or she will encounter many things in the course of writing, is called upon to *open up* and *expand* that which is by definition hidden and restricted, in the world and in him- or herself.

My second answer to those who are unable to accept that to write is to engage in self-discovery *and* to create literature, is quite simply: *this is what I am doing.* I am also being called upon to explore the murkier, opaque regions of my own psyche, to explore emotional realms beyond my actual experience, and to tease and wrestle with language so that it will stand as an adequate world in its own right. These processes are concurrent, and are so for most of the writers and many hundreds of students I have worked with over 25 years.

I am both changed and developed by writing and am changing and developing myself and others in the process. My emotional, intellectual and spiritual landscape is always on the move. I have had times that could be called traumatic, and times of breakthrough. But I am the fuller for it and have more of myself and the world 'at play' to work with.

At the same time I am writing and producing 'literature' – poems, prose pieces, short stories, novels. To write is to risk, challenge, encounter. To write is to extend the phrase 'to be alive'. To write is to make something called literature. The word 'therapeutic' is for me so much a given part of the process that I almost dislike bringing it into the light and implying therefore that it is a separate process needing separate consideration.

These things are sensed in the activity itself and proved in its regular recurrence. It is often with surprise, even shock, that one can look back on the work of writing a piece and realize that one may have entered the mind of a child, flown like a bird, felt the grip of relentless hatred in pummelling the chair with a fist or eaten an unknown delicious fruit.

Every human being has capacities of experience, imagination and expression which are not being released under current social conditions. I hope this book will be as various as my dozen eccentric writers and friends once were for me and that whatever vacuum is your particular *bête noire*, you will be able to close its huge mouth with a stream, or even a torrent of words.

Practice

Much of this is taken from my earliest 'lessons':

a) Invent a jungle and then explore it.
b) Work on what has been spoiled.
c) You can be magpie, thief, voyeur, fly-on-the-wall, hunter.
d) You can juggle, mimic, excavate, insult, get high, blaspheme, disguise.
e) You can borrow from the other arts, be: actor, photographer, sculptor, dancer, singer, musician, film-maker, collage-artist.

Try out the following, giving yourself a time-limit of five minutes/ten minutes:
1) Collect a number of verbal scraps on the page. Don't try to link them. Put them there and let them make their own connection. (Patchwork, collage.)
2) Invent a scene, any scene, giving yourself three elements:
   a) a character; b) a place; c) an object.

Repeat this with another scene altogether, choosing a different set of three elements.

Do not write down the links between scene 1 and scene 2.

Imagine what might have happened to get the viewer (reader) from scene 1 to scene 2. (Making movies.)

3) Go for a walk. Snoop. Look through the cracks in walls. Jot down what you see. Don't fill it out literally. Bring the notebook home and extend what you have into a longer piece, using your own associations. (Magpie, voyeur.)

And so on.

4 WE NEVER DID MAKE IT TO JERUSALEM

The farther a man follows the rainbow, the harder it is for him to get back to the life which he left starving like an old dog.
Jane Bowles, *The Peter Owen Anthology*

There are many methods of release, growth and healing on offer. Possibly hundreds of invitations to take a particular route and end up somewhere else – a process of transformation. These methods belong to something called 'the alternative sector'. Which is itself a questionable phrase since if we choose a particular action or direction it is by definition as an alternative to something else.

I would in any case take issue with a number of alternative practices for one prime reason: that any system of belief or path to well-being which sets out to simplify matters, to reduce our complexity and range, is both failing to give human beings their full due and at the same time is creating an image to aspire to. This, in most cases, will be limited in scope and so create in its shadow a repository for all our troublesome areas. Like having a permanent builder's skip outside the house where we can conveniently dump and displace our rubbish.

Many invitations seem to say: become something else, transform yourself and you'll be all right. Whereas I'm saying the opposite: you're all right as you are, only use and release what's buried there. I see the former of these enterprises as a kind of insult to people's richness and diversity.

A practice which does not embrace the shaping power of language in its fidelity to diversity can actively curtail knowledge in stopping short of words. A kind of foreclosure of what it is in our power to find.

Let's look closer at the assumptions at play here so that we can see what's really on offer.

Most practices involve the idea of harmony and suggest that engaging in a particular activity will lead to a condition of equilibrium. As though the ironing-out of fluctuations were the best possible outcome. A kind of psychic lobotomy, no trouble.

Inherent in this lies the idea of a Promised Land, an 'elsewhere' that will be free from conflict, struggle and all the so-called unpleasant emotions. And inherent in this is an implied directive that where you are now and all that is contained therein, is to be rejected or dismissed in favour of another place (or condition of being) which will involve the shedding of much of what you are. Rather than *using*, translating or processing it. (Drugs are 'utopia' in this sense also.)

Having experimented with a number of practices and numerous intoxicating substances over several decades, I can say from the heart that I'm glad I never did make it to Jerusalem. I've written a short story by this name which deals with a literal proposed journey to the Promised Land and how things kept getting in the way of take-off – the death of the narrator's stepfather, her friend Mo's crisis, an unpleasant encounter with a hairdresser who did the hair of the women in the terraces in their own home. Irritants, you may think. Extraneous details preventing what ought to have happened.

My story persuaded me to think of it in another way. Or rather, thinking of it in another way gave rise to the story. These interventions, interruptions to my narrator's chosen essential journey to reach an 'elsewhere' became the very material of her life and so of my writing. And in being grasped in this way, transformed into rich pickings. The 'rejected' life was indeed alive and kicking, in all its rags and tatters.

And we can see this as a metaphor not only for the 'elsewhere' of a geographical move (which may in fact have nothing to do with a utopian search) but for the elsewhere involved in any *short-cut* method of physical or mental change with a defined arrival-point.

Aspects of the health movement can be seen as almost dangerous in this respect. The purification and toning of the body, health as attached to the image of a prime condition in the physical sense, has unpleasant associations with the master-race ideology of Nazi Germany. First the Jews and gypsies, then the so-called 'deformed'. I sense a whiff of fascism embedded within many alternative life-styles and cultures. It disturbs me. What of the percentage of the population who lack speech or hearing or movement of limb? Limitation belongs to us all and 'lack' is a relative thing depending on what you are comparing it with. For me, writing is the most egalitarian of activities. It claims no special abilities – entry to a purer realm, acquisition of a superior state of mind or physique. For the material is valid in whatever form. Our interest lies not in aspiration to a 'better' common form, but in the very variety, the unique individuality of each practitioner. The release, growth and expression of a human being's life might lie in another approach altogether. The unlocking of inner space and outer space in one. Not in order to avoid the myriad overlapping universes that lie coiled up in there, but to do business with all of them.

For how much closer to the condition of freedom lies the man or woman who has the courage to take on and *manage* all aspects of their nature. And in letting loose on the page in the specific differentiated reality of verbal language the vast arena of their lives and histories, relationships and visions.

How can this happen if we inhale or swallow a substance to remove the dark? To *induce* what we would better find by our own planning and investigation?

Don't misunderstand me. I have every respect for the journeys that are taken on which may involve a 'return' to an earlier and perhaps more primitive state of consciousness. As long as we realize that such states of being are re-entered for the purpose of return and resumption of our fuller and conscious humanity. Within the writing practice we may even find that such states are entered by way of our word-play, since the evocative power of language is equivalent to any other form of image stimulus. But image there must be. I have been witness to many distressing situations when, for example, a weekend encounter-workshop (run by an alternative-therapy practitioner, a theatre group, whatever) has 'successfully' taken a number of people into contact with or immersion in undifferentiated reality. Has 'broken down' their normal defences in the name of the necessity of shedding the self, the identity, as though the collapse of these were essential to health or enlightenment. The practitioners are then plunged into 'somewhere else'. In which state of being they have been subject to the random bombardment of nightmare and near-formless landscapes and presences which are the stuff of terror and chaos when met in that way. Such people – some of whom have spoken to me at great length of this – have found themselves out on the street, back on the train or home again, with the sudden release having been 'overwhelming' and nothing remaining but confusion, anxiety and a collision of worlds so all-embracing that they have become the victims of healing and not its master. (Remember Humpty Dumpty.)

And a sense of failure. You are told that the relinquishing of your identity is to enter a superior state of being, that you are restricted and impoverished all the while you are 'imprisoned' by your ego, your 'self'. You can't handle it when it starts to happen. However kind and perceptive the group's leader, you have failed. You didn't make the grade. In some cases, people have felt they must have something terribly wrong with them to be so unable to cope.

There is another aspect to this also: the condition of transcendence or 'high' may not have been terrible but euphoric. So much so that there is no inducement to continue at all with ordinary life. With anything.

I believe that the close and meticulous engagement with self and world that writing involves will value the self across the whole spectrum of its doing *here and now*. May create the very opposite of rêverie or euphoria in an excitement of another kind. But in so dong will increase the capacity for active involvement, will encourage the restless, searching and investigative spirit and have far more to do with revealing the miraculous than any of the proliferation of 'elsewheres' on offer.

Writing keeps hold of the material world in which, whatever our spiritual belief, or lack of it, we are required to live for the time being. And in that span granted to us, I find it more fulfilling to think of myself as an explorer of all that is contained herein than working within the reductionist terms of energy-transmission, for example, and the like.

Energy is always and ever zapping through our world and ourselves by means of material form. It is always coloured, shaped and defined by the objects it gives rise to.

So also with language. We can only be sharing this at all because I am writing words on a page in various and diverse combinations. In so doing I express my life and belief within the field of relationship that includes you and me.

The importance of this lies in the sometimes hidden assumption that 'word' and what it stands for are separate things. They are not. They are woven together inexorably, even when we invent them.

To write for life is thus becoming clearer when we see that the liberation and expansion this gives us is not a ticket to ride elsewhere. Rather, it is a promise of another order altogether: to realize the ambiguous and multi-dimensional nature of ourselves and the world as 'here', and in that realization to be confronted with a growing sense of *choice*.

This is what word-use gives us. No definite, fixed thing that we aim at as though it were an altar in a building designated for that purpose. Rather permission to dispense with such notions altogether and open up the far riskier idea that there are not only a million landscapes but also a million routes through them and an equivalent variety of means of travel.

Heady stuff, but better surely to hold the idea of a prize which is continuing process than the disappointment of an 'answer' – the finality and closure of the Promised Land.

Postscript

Another way in might be to suggest that we've been wrong in this and in attaching certain myths to the term 'Promised Land'. We might instead try to redefine its meaning. After all, I *am* holding out a carrot. Only saying that my carrot, my Promised Land, will rapidly develop the habit of suggesting also the entire vegetable kingdom, and then the various cooking habits we have known, and so the population of kitchens – and so on it goes. It is as though the fixed phrase or object *cannot* stay within its own skin. Like the contents of the world itself, it must needs interact, connect with its neighbour.

Practice

1) Make a list of your own 'Promised Lands' (three or four). Imagine the space you are sitting in now transformed into one of the places you'd prefer. Then another.

   What is it like?

   What values or meaning lie in its new form?

2) Explore in words the space you are in now.
   a) Like a detective.
   b) Close your eyes: without sight.
   c) Play some music. What does it do to the space and the things contained in it?

3) Take a carrot and place it in front of you.
   a) What are the associations you have with this carrot?
   b) Let these associations take you elsewhere.

You can repeat these writings each day for one week.

   Or take one for each day.

   Or do all of them on a certain day each week for four weeks.

5 WHAT LIES WITHIN THE MOMENT'S NOTE?

The emotionally upset adolescent or middle-aged woman will follow poetry because it is the only immediately available mode of expressing, exploiting and dignifying emotional disturbance. The spectacle is often both absurd and bewildering.

Robin Skelton, *The Practice of Poetry*

Writing ... is an important way for humanity to regain itself.

Michael Longley, heard on *Time for Verse*, Radio 4, 3 June 1991

It may be that a state of paralysis or non-action can occur because one is holding an unconscious ideal: I want to change everything all at once. If I can't change everything all at once, there's no point in doing anything at all. This is based on an insistence on perfection and on a finished product which is perfect. 'Perfection' and 'perfect' being of course dependent upon any one person's ideal.

I prefer a rather different idea: I wish to change or help this situation/person/environment. If I act *within this moment* I will cause change. I will *make a difference.*

It is rather like what happens in the healing professions when the nurse, occupational therapist or therapist may weep at the end of the day because he or she can't restore her patient to 'normal'. And in this reaction, input is always being measured and valued against the notion of 'wholeness' or 'normality'.

Suppose we reverse this idea or start from a different place altogether. Here is a patient who can't see on the left side, only on the right. I can widen that seeing to include a little more or I can help him to achieve *more* with what seeing he does have.

Do we really want to hold the attitude that lack or disturbance or limitation disqualifies a human being from having as valuable experience and expression as anyone else? Within our current social system, guided by our esteemed representatives, it would seem so. We are moving very fast in Britain towards a society where such divisions will be so entrenched that they are virtually irreversible.

So let us, for preference, represent ourselves.

Suppose we now relate this directly to writing. I wish to change the world. I may weep that the novel (poem, letter, scrawl) which I have written does not appear to have changed the world. *Or* I can say this book, page, back-of-an-envelope has made real, or marked out, what did not exist before – both in my own mind and memory (storehouse) and 'out there' in the world separate from me.

Let's hold in mind the heading of this chapter – what lies within the moment's note – also the two quotations, and think about the moment of postponing and suspending that goes on if we hold to the notion of 'ideal conditions'. If we are waiting on the weather, time of day, clearance, free time, conjunction of the planets, illumination in ourselves and so forth, we will clearly be waiting unto death. And I believe most strongly that the enterprise of postponement, if it is deeply rooted, is one that only death can satisfy in its complete absence of stimulation, distraction, anything that moves. It is surely fear that makes us wait. Fear of what we'll meet if we turn back from our turning-away and begin with what we have now. In changing our minds on this particular front, we may perhaps need to meet our arch-enemy and do business with him also. Allow the accompaniment of fear, until we get our bearings in the here-and-now. And learn to cope with what I've come to call 'the extravagance of being there'.

It works both ways. We can't begin to write because the grip of our belief that *we are not in a fit state* or the environment is not 'fitting' is too strong. And because whatever lies within our reach will always be the starting-point, then we have entirely prevented that beginning in assuming that some future moment must be the starting-point. And what lies *within* may be too painful, untidy, unmanageable and out of control. And I mean this both when we are working with the emotions or more objectively in the work of capture of what lies more explicitly outside ourselves.

If we read Robin Skelton as our temporary manifesto as to what writing is and how it serves us, we are clearly unfit! And why only adolescent, middle-aged and female? The assumption and directive here are preposterous. What emotional disturbance, if any, occurs between adolescence and middle age? I assume he means the particular emotional quality of menstruation and menopause. Emotions at such times, if wedded to insight, can produce extraordinary expansions.

And what of men, and their emotions?

Any emotional condition is clearly, for Skelton, undignified. It is a spectacle. It is absurd, it is bewildering. To be moved, it seems. To be in something other than an emotion*less*, detatched and rarefied frame of mind.

And once again we see how words can claim and clamp us. Lock us within their frame. (Their frame-of-mind.)

I will choose some more as an act of resistance. But also less stridently, to restore most carefully to their rightful place our damaged lives, our overspill, our wounds and losses. And we will find in there the very means to proceed. Right at the dreaded core of our extremes, the love that will lodge a shape, maybe a hand or face, sunlight on our dusty surfaces, a creased cushion. The *prints* of our life here. Which, I stress again, is both given to us and is forged *by* us to work with.

It is cold. Men are drilling in the road. Those shoes you bought in a bargain-sale pinch like hell after all. The second post brings a bill and a reminder to vote. You don't give a damn. You'll start tomorrow. Nothing can help. *You don't want it to.* The leaden lump of flesh that is you *will not* budge from its stupor.

Now, you must resist.

It is only an idea you hold, that you cannot write in bad weather. Whether it's a sodden grey mist outside or a mean-spirited mind, lying inert and resentful as far away from the stove as it can get. Just to prove a point.

It is only an idea you hold. The wrong time of the month, they call it?

You must resist. In my introduction, I mentioned my life-journey, its faithful and *treacherous* storehouse, as the core material for going on. If you take on board the second quotation at the beginning of this chapter, you may travel far in this gloom, this half-seen.

But to make a journey, it is necessary to begin. Whether or not you see your life as blessed with good fortune, what you have known are riches, many-textured. If you live in the inner city, or a country retreat, gather the details, collect them as objects or words as a magpie does. They will begin to speak back.

Practice

Here it is necessary to stretch a little. Work over a longer time.

Concentrate on observing or becoming aware, of how you are feeling, how the day seems.

Perhaps allow half an hour each morning. Or if this is impractical, at some other time during the day or evening. Or certain days in the week.

But make a commitment.

And take each, in turn, of the conditions that make you *postpone*. Ones that I have mentioned and any more that are your own. Either biological – specific pain or general malaise. Or 'external', such as noise, bad weather, good weather, bad news, state of the planet.

Note them down, as I might in my room today.

a) It's cold.
b) Men are drilling in the road.
c) New shoes I can't wear, they pinch.
d) All that *comes in* is a bill, a demand that I pay. And a reminder to vote, what does it mean and what power does it give me?
e) The leaden lump of flesh that is me.

In each case, write of it, extend it, address it.

a) Dig into the cold, find out exactly what it is doing. The force or influence of it. Make the cold like a live thing, a creature, that creates all kinds of transformations. Tell it what to do. Love it. Hate it. Go into it, protect yourself from it. All on the page.
b) What of the drill? What is it doing? Explore its intrusion. Speak to the men. What does it *do* to you, remind you of, what is it like?

c) Make the shoes alive. As though they are deliberately hurting you. Avenging themselves? Speak to them. Extend the scene when you bought them. What were you doing? What were the dreams and fantasies attached to and arising from buying these shoes? Where would they take you and how would you travel?

d) Explore the hardness of figures. The money. What is it like, this bill, with its straight lines and columns? How does it measure and cut up the world? And you?

What man or woman sent it, in her malice? Explore the threat, the sense of force, trap, of money, owing it.

Vote: what will he/she do for you if elected? What would you like her to do? Fantasize! Imagine you could have anything.

Redemption

In the cold, pain, noise, disappointment, imagine something most loved, most beautiful to *you*. Make a journey on the page. Travel slowly through these difficulties and slowly the loved one emerges ahead of you. Write it.

In all cases keep alive the *associations* that arise from your core subject, *your* equivalent to my: COLD, DRILL (MEN), SHOES, BILL, POLITICAL PAMPHLET.

6 INVITATIONS

I wonder when there was last a British Government whose idea of the human being and of human society is as low as yours has been.

David Constantine (poet), *Letters to Margaret Thatcher*, *Guardian*
15 August 1990

At every turn, in every corner of the High Street and in every nook and cranny of the planet, you are being issued with invitations. All are sent out to encourage you to approach, choose, acquire, and for involvement of some kind. Some of these invitations are cloaked in such language that you are persuaded at once tha: you cannot do without this product, exercise, treatment, course of action. In buying what it is you are invited to buy, you are automatically acquiring an image of yourself.

The way invitations are issued can come close to coercion or seduction. It is difficult to see the dividing-line between the hard sell and an offering whereby you are also provided with space to consider. Many invitations call upon your drive towards immediate gratification and may be exerting a horrendously powerful magnetism upon you unconsciously, hitting those areas which have not relinquished the child's expectation of quick results. In the language of the market economy, you want to show a quick profit and this is in your best interests.

Whatever the country and its political climate, the possibilities exist for emphasis on the satisfaction of more infantile desires. This process may be disguised, so that people 'learn' or acquire a short attention-span as part of themselves and lose the ability to cope with a longer-term perspective. Even our news stories on television hardly ever linger on any item long enough for more considered involvement and the involvement of our own discriminatory activity.

This creates the conditions for a gullible and needy population to emerge who are primed not to think too hard. Not weigh and measure in anything other than a framework of speed, efficiency and monetary results

Within the market, miracles are possible. You can, you *might* get rich quick. There is the proof of those who have. Within some areas of alternative culture, miracles appear to be possible under the influence of cure-all life-styles and practices. The promises of use, of engaging in these rituals are much the same:

- The avoidance of meaningful activity for you.
- The elevation of a struggle-free existence.
- Instant turn-on, disguised as change.

• You don't have to think for yourself, since what's on offer is a mindless allegiance to forces beyond your control. (The market has a mind of its own; the planets rule your destiny; a joint will make you believe make-believe.)

There are only a few minutes to wait. You sit back and *let it happen.*

You are made virtuous in your passivity.

In all these cases you are changing your mind in one sense only: closing most of it down.

The invitation to engage in writing practice is in part to bring into view the hidden mechanisms of daily communication. To take up the choice we perhaps don't know we have, of using language for expansion *or* prevention. To see to begin with how we collude without knowing it in our further diminishment.

Collude also in a utilitarian shorthand which renders the world sterile (the language of the economy); or renders the world diffuse (the language of enlightenment and transcendence).

My invitation therefore is to make those very areas of pain, doubt and perhaps shame, which other invitations promise to remove, the very centre of your engagement. And I *mean* the dis-ease, the monsters, the blasphemous. Let these be also your starting-points, places of ignition. Some of the finest, strongest writing comes from the blackest of sources. Our nightmarish dreams that don't make sense, take on a potency, a vibrant shape, when written and used as raw material. Where we are troubled is as much a source of power as when we dance for pleasure.

Society is set upon a clean-up job. A sanitized world where no nasty bugs can get in. Some of our century's greatest writers have satirized this. Politicians promise this. The thrust of Western development is based on providing its peoples with greater ease. In this cleaner world, pollution is dumped elsewhere. And the so-called undeveloped nations are so undernourished that their own rituals and wisdoms are forgotten, sliding out of sight beneath the great bulldozer of Western advancement and sales drive.

It is important to take a look at these connections. We are persuaded that our ease and gratification are desirable, necessary and inevitable. Whether it's a crystal ball or a bank-note, a pill or a theme park.

Let's look at the individual in the same terms as a nation: if you insist on a cleansed mind or imagination, you'll sure as hell dump the pile-up of waste on someone else's doorstep. And just as importantly, you'll lose out on the joy of claiming your own multiple landscapes. And be in danger from those guests to whom you refuse entry, creeping in much later – unseen and uninvited – by the back door.

The invitation here is of another order altogether: to discover and manage a greater variety of movement; to expand and introduce some new tools to live with; to struggle with the precarious but none the less concrete building-blocks of our already-known vocabulary; to change the *parameters* of your language-use and so your life and practice; to slowly come to terms (to terminology) with your feared, forbidden malevolence/malpractice and use its fertility; to move towards a greater knowledge and use of that gift which is in danger of being stunted in its infancy (nipped in the bud), language; to discover and invent different ways of being alive; to use language differently towards a greater humanization.

In other words to trade in a single, fixed view of the way the world is and you are *not* for another clearly defined alternative but for space and means to choose many other alternatives. As though you have been let loose in a vast walk-in wardrobe of costume disguises gathered together from all the theatres, pantomimes, operas, designer-studios, film-sets and weaving-sheds on the entire planet. And you can try them on at will, you are free to do so. But you'll have to be willing to take off what you are wearing now, say no to your usual persona, way of dressing. And perhaps shiver at first in that time of nakedness before the next outfit leads you to stand differently (you may be on stilts) or see the word upside-down (clowns tumble). And knowing how close the smile and the tears are in a clown's make-up.

Practice

A number of key ideas emerge in this section: each can involve you in a writing response.

1) *Resistance.* I recommend David Constantine's letter and others like it. Write a letter to your Prime Minister or President. No prescriptions as to the tone or content.

2) Imagine a garden or the corner of a garden.
   a) Focus on its wilderness and disorder and write about it from that point of view.
   b) Tidy it up, focus on its cleanliness and order. Write about it from that point of view.
   Concentrate as always on the details.
   Do the same with a room.

3) Imagine a product or a course of activity which is claimed to change people's lives.
   a) Write an advertising blurb for it, an 'invitation'.
   b) Imagine a situation where you have tried it out and it doesn't work. Write a letter of complaint to the manager or manufacturer or organizer.
   Don't be afraid to exaggerate or push it to absurdity.
   Don't worry about sticking to 'the truth'.
   Or to invent a product or course of action you've never seen on offer.

4) Choose a landscape, interior or exterior. A 'corner' of town or countryside.
   a) Write of it in the language of a business report and economic value.
   b) Write about it in the language of sensual pleasure (all senses).
   Is it the same place? Is your mind the same?

Government such as yours is really a belittling of the human being ... People are more generous – more imaginative ... than you ever gave them credit for.

David Constantine, *Letter to Margaret Thatcher*

7 THE EXTRAVAGANCE OF BEING THERE

Meander if you want to get to town.

Michael Ondaatje

If you haven't been living at the fullest extent of yourself, the idea of self-possession meaning the admission of all possible aspects of yourself can seem like an extravagance, a possibly absurd luxury. But I use the word deliberately and with approval, for it is the luxury we have the greatest right and claim to.

Writing is a means of reaching for and attaining the fullest life and presence for yourself and thus achieving for yourself a new sense of potency.

In the course of my work, I've found over and over again that potency can be restored by the admission of *more* to the awareness and so to the imaginative faculty. Even if painful and difficult.

That impotence often lies in a grim closure at the heart. This cannot be unlocked all at once. I've mentioned the dangers of sudden and absolute 'letting-in'. The step-by-step process of writing can come to be a gradual reclaiming of one's life and potential which has somehow got left out in the rush. The directive coming from the social machine outside ourselves, to travel ever faster, use words in a certain way, accumulate ever more, soon becomes a drive which one imposes on oneself. We don't need external policing. We have ourselves acquiesced in our own slavery in this respect.

We can come to be so disempowered that alternatives can seem fearful.

Now you may ask, what exactly do I mean by 'the extravagance of being there' and what is this extravagance?

Firstly, I insist that I do not mean a condition of bliss. Nor do I advise turning one's back on economics, opting out, dropping out and turning on. I did all that in the sixties and early seventies and it led me up a blind alley whereby I came dangerously close to being unable to *do* anything at all.

I'm proposing something more complex than that. I'm talking about what is actually contained in any one moment of one's life, yet is obscured and at the same time potential.

Now, *obscured* means that something exists there, but it's hidden or out-of-sight, in the corners of the mind. This 'something' is everything that isn't immediately present to the awareness. And we are accustomed and encouraged to live within a narrow and in fact diminishing awareness-field. To choose to focus on this can have extraordinary results. Proust's novel *Remembrance of Things Past* begins with the memory from his childhood of the smell of the cakes served at tea with his grandmother. Catching this smell later in life, he wove his masterpiece from one moment. In a sense, a whole life was contained in that one, re-created *actual* sensation. Extravagance, richness, potentiality are contained not so much in memory as in memory's literal recovery as sensation. The texture of wood, the flimsy worn quality of ancient cloth, the sizzling pink plastic of a cocktail stick. Any one of these gathers associations. A scene is built which then has its own pressure to expand. See how our awareness is widened out on the page as we seek the significances that lie behind and within our chosen object or sensation.

In contrast, and looking at this strictly linguistically, certain tabloid newspapers would be examples of an extremely limited view of human nature and awareness. To remind you of one of the worst excesses, I quote that well-known headline which appeared in a newspaper here after the British invasion of the Falklands in 1992. The Argentinian cruise-ship turned vessel of war, the *Belgrano*, was judged to be lying inside the exclusion zone marked out by Britain and was sunk with a single missile. 'GOTCHA!' covered virtually the entire front page. This slogan influenced, seduced or bullied some of the British people into an attitude which kept out of sight full knowledge of the horror of that event, lives lost, just as effectively as the ship itself had been 'taken out' as a cover-word for sunk, bombed, crushed, destroyed. We kill as surely with our words and the shaping of our minds by them, as we kill with bombs and rifles. David Constantine writes:

I am bound to believe that human beings in Britain now are capable of reading things more humane and imaginative and intellectually challenging than the *Sun* newspaper. That is why, whatever texts I teach and without ever mentioning you and your colleagues by name, my teaching is necessarily an act of opposition.

(Letter to Margaret Thatcher)

There's a danger of rejoicing in the *certainty* that slogans can temporarily provide, whether the subject is war, or an individual target for media attention. (Witness the excess of nationalism of the victory parades.)

Extravagance reclaims our right to fullest knowledge and involvement with ourselves; with our environment (both near and far, domestic and global); with our own and others' history; with the resonance and meaning that metaphor and association can give us and which can so profoundly alter our relationship to the objects and living things that inhabit our vicinity; with our expectations, intentions and desires; with our emotional, intuitive and mental condition at any time we want to look at it.

You, in your present moment, have access to all this. We can see that 'being there' may be a bare fact, stripped of its context – or can be a tremendous hive of presences and possibilities. This is neither a simple, easy nor safe option.

I have said that there is contained in the present moment both the obscured and the potential. The obscured is 'there' but hidden. So one route is to set out with the aim of *revealing*. But the 'potential' lies also hidden within the act of discovery. Any moment of revealing involves also choice and intervention. We 'select' this or that, the mind and imagination working at super-conscious speed. We arrange, connect and so create an entity. So a 'memory' is composed of scraps and fragments that have sprung into life in us, involuntarily. Is also composed of those elements we have searched for and the construction and invention we bring to bear. The potential is what we may do in setting it all in motion and also what we may do with the material that then emerges.

If you think of all this happening within any moment of questioning, searching or desiring, then extravagance is the right word after all. So rich and associative can be the single moment that it can enlarge to infinity. We are always sitting on a minefield, a treasure trove or a volcano. Slowly out it will come from its buried places. We are excavating and inventing the world and ourselves together. Self-possession now carries a little more weight than we first thought.

Language meanders, apparently off-course, in order to return to us a redeemed and restored present moment. Only language is adequate to the specific intricacy of experience – that curious cloth woven of different time-spans, weathers and textures. Can dig even closer and give us the connection in all its sharp detail.

We all carry memory, areas of our past with a certain tone or colour to them. Amorphous and distant when we first approach, language can call back those lost times and bring them to vivid life. The moment then reveals itself not as an isolated and separate thing, but as bursting with history and the anticipation of what is to come.

'Meander if you want to get to town.' Town is where it's at, the heart of it. Or the core of you.

Where the action is.

Practice

1) Memory: bring it close.
   a) Take a moment of your past. Stay with it. Write down all that you see there. What each element then suggests.

      See how it springs into life, like sharpening the focus on a lens.
   b) Make a list of ten specific images or fragments from your memory. Concentrate on detail. If you write a vague phrase, ask yourself, 'What is it really like, what is it like *exactly*?'

      eg my father in the bathroom = first memory.

      Response: 'My father, face very red, clutching the *News of the World*. Looming out of steam. Stranger suddenly. I bolt and bury myself under the eiderdown. His feet wet on the lino. Quilt like a house', etc.

2) GOTCHA!
   a) Write an alternative. Go behind the slogan. Don't worry about accuracy. A small event or moment on the *Belgrano*. Invent what you don't know.
   b) Take a headline from a newspaper. Do the same. Humanize, take your time. Go in close. Explore. As though you are the lens, but capable of empathy.

3) The moment.
Take three aspects:
   a) immediate environment (associate);
   b) what's on your mind (past);
   c) what's on your mind (future).
   See how the ripples spread outwards.
   What is the furthest point in space and time these associations take you to?

8 SAFE HOUSES

As a form of expression, writing cannot help being an exploration and discovery of one's own consciousness and psychology as well as being an entity in itself, a separate and created 'thing'. Even the notebook forms, the first drafts, have always had this dual nature for me and sometimes my own early clusters of notes return to me as marvels. (*Not* as great writing!) I am caught unawares by the vividness and power of these raw beginnings. Whether or not they will ever be worthy of publication is another matter.

I want to look at power in both its positive and negative aspects and see how writing practice can contribute to the diffusing of negative power and the translating of negative into positive.

Let us think of writing as a 'safe house' for the moment. A place between fantasy and actuality, a place where activity can happen which has an element of catharsis. But is also in some sense a substitute for, on the one hand, a spiralling into morbidity that can happen when negative emotions take hold – when one turns one's negativity upon oneself for want of proper outlet. Or, at the other extreme, a burst into expression of bottled-up violent feeling which might do damage to oneself or others.

Art has always been a creative space for that which defies expression elsewhere. If we turn this round, we could say that art might be a creative space for that which *ought not* to find expression elsewhere.

It can be looked at in two ways. One could say that a violent book will incite its readers to violence; or one can say that there is some form of relieving of one's attraction to violence if the journey is taken in the hands of a skilful author. We come through the experience, extend and explore without needing to act it out in the world.

In certain cultures, theatre and performance officially and intentionally fulfil this very function – to ritualize, and so cleanse the people of what might otherwise release in an arbitrary and damaging fashion. This must involve an acceptance that destructive forces exist within us all and not just in everyone else! It's what we do with them that counts.

I've said that power has positive and negative aspects. The desire for power is negative in its aspect of power *over* others, positive in its aspect of increasing one's power for one's self and power to manage all that one can be and realize. We can be reasonably certain that desire for power over others will arise from a projection on to them of 'enemy' combined with a sense of impotence in oneself; if this is not admitted, a man or woman can go to considerable lengths to maintain whatever mechanisms they have set up for the denial of their own vulnerability and violence, and be driven as though by a nameless force to seek effect in the world around them and the people in it. That effect being to *reduce* or *control* what's around them, and not using their power to facilitate release.

I've many writer friends who've told me of their own negative drives and how their obsessions and sometimes violent fantasies would have been utterly destructive in their lives had they not shaped and channelled these forces into fictional or poetic space. We know also that actors when needing to instantly display (or realize) an extreme emotion, will often call upon an incident in their own lives of an equivalent emotional charge. To tap directly the source within themselves and so create something real and moving.

It is no different for the writer. It's important to be willing to ride the emotional spectrum and admit it within oneself. But in the company of pen and page, the experience need not be mindless and out-of-control. But filtered, sifted, whittled and directed into place.

There is all the difference between the deliberate use of images in documentary propaganda and the indirect placing of images to create poems and stories.

The use of images by the Nazis in their attack on the Jewish population was powerful indeed. Techniques of persuasion which use conjunction of image and idea for their effect. For example, shots of rats scrambling through sewers, while raving against the Jews in the commentary. This technique is powerful and persuasive and *changes people's minds*. All images, visual or written, have the power to do this. Any writing, therefore, is a tool for the power of persuasion. But the use of images for a single purpose, to incite prejudice and hatred, is not the same activity as the use of images to explore and invent and to create thereby a whole fictional scene which will itself have further context and take its place in an ongoing process. The latter has built into it the open space. The former closes any space whatsoever. The Nazi propaganda films, and all other propaganda methods, close the world into an absolute diktat. Poetry and fiction do not judge and finalize in this way. Which is why I talk of writing as 'holding the world open'. Open for consideration and speculation for the reader, *within the text itself.*

An extreme example on a collective level of psychological processes remaining unaddressed and unrecognized, is the move to war. In an English newspaper during 1991 there appeared a letter from over 100 supporters of the Medical Campaign Against Nuclear Weapons, opposing the threatened war in the Gulf. 'We believe that the rush to war is largely driven by irrational psychological processes which must be recognized and addressed if sanity is to prevail.'

There is only a difference of degree between the results of unacknowledged and denied aggressions within one person or an entire nation. Collectively and politically, these aggressions lead to national conflict. Some of the irrational processes are listed as follows:

> An intergroup process which involves each side exaggerating its own virtues and the other side's capacity for evil.
>
> The denial of reality when it is felt to be too painful to face eg the threatened devastation of war.
>
> Aggressive impulses may only be seen in other individuals or groups, not in one's own self or group.
>
> The search for an outside 'enemy' when there are difficult domestic realities to deal with.
>
> A tendency to (desire to) replace feelings of fear, persecution and depression with those of worth, success and triumph, even if the latter are based on a delusion, such as the possibility of 'winning' a war.
>
> The extreme difficulty of bearing uncertainty, particularly over time, leads to pressure to act impulsively and precipitately.
>
> Letter from Medical Campaign Against Nuclear Weapons,
> *The Guardian*, 16 January 1991

All these examples of what is at play on a collective psychological level in the build-up to war (much the same could be said of the rise of fascism in Germany in the thirties) can apply equally to individual psychological processes leading to a single violent act.

But what if we were to exorcize our demons in an imaginary or constructed world? Perhaps then there might be less of a drive to act out our hates externally and lessen our need continually to manifest control over the external world and its people.

You might think I'm trying to suggest that the ills of the world will be solved if the entire planet sits down and writes. That would be absurd. I'm merely pointing to an aspect and use of the writing process which is not at the front of people's minds: that it is a way of increasing our internal space, channelling our drives and emotions, ritualizing the sometimes frightening play of forces within us which we need to suppress most of the time in order to be 'acceptable' to society. And I need to remind myself quite often of the thresholds that my writing has helped me to cross and the threshold that much of my writing *is*, whether or not it reached the printed page.

Dreams are safe houses.

So are therapeutic spaces, whether an hour, a day, a week. Also theatres, dances and some rites of passage. Children are allowed safe houses in their guided play. They are spaces where it is possible to avoid the twin trap of being in prison with all of yourself within your own mind and/or driven to act blindly and destructively in the 'real' world. Spaces where it is possible to create a reflection of who and what you are and what you are doing, *really* doing, and so do business with yourself. And thus more wisely with others.

They are all places of process, assimilation, digestion. An out-of-time or an in-between where what was hidden is called into view. Accepted and worked with, however long it takes. It's a pity there aren't more of such times and spaces, officially sanctioned, available to everyone. Perhaps more of the adult population could let out their unresolved infantile drives (for absolute power and/or boundless nurture) and play the matter out instead of starving, killing and maiming their own kind. I don't see creative writing as replacing all other processes. But therapeutic processes can be expensive and/or inaccessible to many people, or only available on an occasional basis. Frequent engagement with writing will always create movement and facilitate awareness. Try it, in conjunction with other processes or as a valuable alternative. You'll be surprised how far it can take you.

Practice

An investigation of power and impotence.

1) The playground. Remember a time of impotence as a child. An incident of shame and helplessness.
   Write how it was.

2) Remember a time when another child was exposed, shamed, helpless.

Write of how it was *for you*.

3) Think of the situation that carries most fear for you. Is most disabling.

Write how it was, is, might be.

4) Think of a situation in which someone else is rendered powerless.

You might try this choosing first someone you love, then someone you hate or fear. Or perhaps it isn't as simple as that – you have love and hate for the same person. In which case write it from the aspect of your love and then the aspect of your fear.

Write how it is for you.

9 THE PROMETHEUS SYNDROME

(My books) ... are about a breakout from confinement, a move towards a better place. But to get there ... you have to confront demons.

Toni Morrison

The poems of heaven and hell have been written, it remains to write the poem of the earth.

Wallace Stevens

There are two forms of invitation to change your mind which are cheating on reality. Prometheus stole fire from the gods as a short-cut to gaining power and vision. He didn't want to activate his own means of attaining these. He was too impatient for that, too lazy. By stealing fire, he would escape those two most necessary constraints – time and effort. Many invitations to change are based upon a Prometheus-like illusion – that if you devote yourself to a particular leader, master, guru, or follow this or that set of instructions, you will be as the gods are. Fire will come into you, you will be 'fired' from elsewhere. This is the invitation which tells you you are deluded and in the dark and if you will only replace your way of seeing with another, or put yourself in the hands of another, then you will change.

Many liberation theories are authoritarian at the root in the sense of claiming the authority and so locating 'authorship' elsewhere.

I feel that any practice which does not allow an extended time for a process of change involving the whole human being and all his/her faculties and gifts, is a false friend. As tricky and sinister in fact as any group or person who holds out the promise of a pain-free world, unlimited safety. That would be to press the person back to an infantile state and *leave them there*. Many fundamentalist religious groups have this tendency and regrettably are increasing their following.

The invitation to change your mind by writing is not of this order. Rather than letting loose a terrifying and chaotic reality – which is what can happen when there is a sudden eruption of unconscious and buried material – writing can loosen *slowly* the fixed boundaries of embedded habit. And the replacement is not a single cohesive alternative *but any number of alternatives*. And you will only know what these are when you begin, since the choices and the material are your own. Your own unique history, encounter and circumstance. Each day's or each moment's choice will be a twisting route, but clearly signposted with events, images and tools for creation.

The invitation is to engage with a facilitator, an enabling process. The entire content is up to you. A constantly repeated invitation to travel within yourself and in the various three-dimensional spaces that the page is offering. To share in the back-and-forth movement between internal and external reality.

Language defines, and so it should. It is essential that it does so. But mysteriously it also releases and it is this two-fold capacity of words that makes them our strongest ally. Either capacity on its own will enslave us: definition will become confinement, the fixed and unarguable absolute of a slogan (political or religious); the open-ended vacuity of an unqualified generalization will enslave within the terror of a boundless lack of feature.

Words are always, thankfully, linked to things and to the material. They expand us into wider experience, to take us heavenwards if you like. But we also have the rope (the tethered kite) to keep us in touch with base. Without words, or with only the words of reduced meaning (Hitler, Stalin, the gods), we are adrift and disempowered.

Writing takes on the value of what I am and say in my own world. In my own particular way, unlike anyone else's.

See what happens when we cheat. Or mistakenly believe that the short-term high in which we may experience an inflated sense of self-worth is a true extension of real value. Is this not a value obtained from taking in, ingesting, the fire from elsewhere rather than beginning with our own spark and ignition (Chapter 1)? And nurturing that which we already have and is our own, into life? And not leaving it at that, but continuing with that self-nurture – and what we do with our own fire – throughout our entire lives?

Let's go back to the question of what lies at the root of our desire, or compulsion, to take on any practice at all. Let's assume that we seek change and movement. So often the easiest and most obvious source of change is to move into a new environment. To 'go out', to 'get out of it'. To put on new clothes so that our body is encased in something different.

So often this kind of movement will let us down. We find that when the effect has worn off, the same sense of futility, dullness, boredom, lack of meaning or whatever, quickly sets in. And then the temptation may be to increase the dose, to take more regularly that means of literal and immediate change of mind.

Either way, we are up a gum tree, as my grandmother put it. We create at once the illusion that the world and ourselves are transformed. We falsely believe that the real deep-rooted change has *in fact* taken place. But further, *we may also falsely believe that* <u>*we*</u> *have achieved it.* In this there are a number of layers of illusion lying close-packed upon one another.

The double damage flies in the face of vision and we end up like Prometheus, in chains. We have created an illusion of growth and expansion and have at the same time damaged and stunted our ability to carry ourselves forward. We are not only stuck but moving backwards.

Let's focus on this: to write is to be or to become a *promoter*, an *initiator*, the author of extension of the world and ourselves. And we take others with us in this action. To hand over this process in any sense is to cancel the enterprise at root. Your action is paramount. Nothing exists to replace it.

The Prometheus story doesn't end, however, with his punishment of being chained to the Caucasus mountains with his liver pecked at by birds, only to heal each day for the next onslaught. Prometheus was acting *for man*, and brought fire to earth for the first time. The story therefore doesn't entirely illustrate my argument! It's used here as an image for a point of view. To work with and to make a point. Images are useful in that they too change and can be used in different ways. Prometheus One is cheating. Prometheus Two takes an enormous risk to provide what was not there before.

Practice

1) What are your associations with fire? Thinking of fire, write a pageful of locations for fire. Think of fire in the literal sense, but also in the sense of 'fired-up', where life ignites, hotting up, etc.

2) What fires you? What makes you burn? Smoulder? Flare up? Blaze?

3) Think of stealing fire from the gods. Now think of fire (passion, energy, heat and light) as located somewhere else or in someone else.

   Write a journey in which you approach and steal it.

10 HOLDING THE WORLD OPEN

Every beggar is a prince of possibility.
George Steiner, *Granta* 36, p. 166

Much of this book and its practice has so far been concerned with the individual writer's own extension and development. I'd like now to introduce another purpose whereby writing fulfils a function also in a wider political sense.

If he or she desires, the writer can create a revolution as effective as any armed force and without destroying life. The writer can do this by giving voices to people (real or invented) who have hitherto been mute. Who are unable to speak for themselves. Who do not have the means – be it channel, skill or motivation.

It is assumed, and often for convenience, that the 'front line' in terms of struggle against regimes that silence and enslave the population, lies overseas. In another country, another continent – anywhere but here. This is convenient in that it absolves us from struggle on our own doorstep. Or it can have an even more subtle effect in leading us to deny that there is anything wrong in our society – that there is no disempowerment, loss of voice, enforced silence.

Irina Ratushinskaya, reading at the Brighton Festival, assumed Britain to be a place of liberty and freedom of speech. By contrast, the Irish poet Damian Gorman, in a television documentary about the conflict in Northern Ireland, spoke of a collusion of silence in the face of atrocity. People gagged by fear, voices silenced by poverty, confusion, deprivation.

Paul Foot has written of words as weapons. Ariel Dorfman in his play *Death and the Maiden* has given voice to a tortured Chilean woman, and her long silence is broken by the writer's *holding open* a space for her to speak. In her speaking she becomes a representative of all who have been so maimed.

I write also to give voices to people who have been silenced. In my novel, *Finding Him*, Archie is physically disabled in his lack of speech, but so acts as a metaphor for a massive dumbness among our own people. For those who have no official 'sanctioned' voice in the community and have lost, or never found, an alternative place of protest. Or celebration. Of what they are, not what they are expected to be.

Writers are able to speak for people who, against the odds and often under appalling conditions, hold to their love and their humanity in the face of their deprivation, reduced as they are.

But I'd rather not speak only of the perspectives and experience of the obviously diempowered. I mean also the so-called privileged, the middle classes, how large areas of their emotional, imaginative lives (their curiosity, their searching) have been cut off and have withered for lack of use. Or people *forced* to use language in a reverse sense, in the service of bureaucracy, efficiency, economy. I have run workshops for secretaries, accountants and lawyers seeking a release from the strait-jacket of their professional language, fearing, often intuitively, that a *capacity* is being irretrievably lost. Often they only find out what it is when we work together and writing reclaims certain dimensions of experience. Or reconnects us to the meaning in our lives and environments.

This can involve the simplest of activities, such as asking each person to imagine a cup, one they have near them or use often. So each person's cup became the carrier for a story, of itself and its user.

If you give life on the page, you give life also to part of yourself. George Steiner tells us that he makes an act of witness and remembrance and memorizes the names of the dead on war memorials. They live on in his speaking of their names. I was unable for a long time to write of my own early family life, its tangles and contradictions. But later – much later – I gave voices to my mother and father. These voices were those that they never could find for themselves, or I could not hear from them at the time. They were the voices of love lost in the noise of daily battle between them. False voices, since they didn't give permission and may never have spoken in this way. But for me, this writing gives them fuller life. I have crept back between them and picked up their currency and given it sound and shape. It is the best I can do, since there is no other way to speak of such things. On our pages, we hold open space for what has been unspoken and may never have spoken. We revive and excavate what can in fact have voice *only here*.

We can go where we choose, put speaking wherever we choose. Chart gestures otherwise unseen – gestures taking place in that private, closed-off space between one person and another. We can give *ourselves* many new voices with our relocation in a life other than our own; a life that we have perhaps touched the edge of. Pretend to be that other person, or thing. In this we are witness and creator of what would otherwise go unmarked, that brotherhood arising from speaking out of ourselves and an other, at the same time.

Take John Berger's essay, 'Miners', at the start of his book *Keeping a Rendez-vous*. A whole community speaks through this single voice, which is Berger's own, and that of a miner at once.

Or the work of Queenspark Books in publishing the stories of people who may never have written in their lives.

Or the hundreds of books that speak from behind bars, from within asylums, from out of the prison of a repressive family life. From behind the locked doors of institutions or simply the faces that are mute closures upon despair. Voices out of forgotten spaces, overlooked corners. I've not forgotten the scene in Barry Unsworth's *Sacred Hunger* when Erasmus Kemp is walking home one night (Liverpool, mid-18th century) and is drawn by a sound coming from an alley and finds an old and stinking creature, a man, near to death and moaning in his extremity. The event is not referred to again until much later in the book when it recurs in the mind of Kemp in another context altogether. Although Barry Unsworth does not give words to his dying man (though he puts words into the minds of many others who do not speak, as we would know it), the presence of the man haunts the pages and is eloquent some 300 pages on when chickens come home to roost, when reckonings are tried and tested.

Official space is a minority interest. To stop and return (as Erasmus does in memory) to that which we had ignored or dismissed in our hurry to get to where the official action is. To go back and prise open, or hold open that which lies at the fringes of society's concerns. Behind the walls of bedsits, prisons or the twitch of a discreet lace curtain.

The activity which we begin with, so private and self-absorbed, is unexpectedly not so private after all.

What we struggle with in our solitude is a supremely public act.

Practice

1) Make a list of moments of dumbness you yourself have experienced. When you have been tongue-tied.

Speak what was going on in that moment. Put the voice in where it couldn't find a way at the time.

2) Think of a mute person, someone in a situation where they cannot or will not speak. From necessity or choice. Speak what they were then unable or unwilling to.

Try a number of such situations. Speak for them in the first person. Address the person who is causing the silence, whether they are present or not in the situation.

11 THE FIRE AND THE ROSE

The business of an artist is to find where God is hiding!
                                                            Pablo Picasso

Transfiguration is what we most desire in the creative process, because this is what unites us with the Creator ...
                                                            Sofia Gubaidulina

It doesn't matter what we call it, the heart of things. Picasso was no saint and probably used the word 'God' to express that which art seeks to uncover and create: the mystery, the core, that which eludes the everyday, utilitarian eye. And to bring out into the open the miraculous. Which is both a way of seeing and the extravagance and quality of the thing seen.

It doesn't matter either whether we believe the world to be a manifestation of the divine or an extraordinary accident. What we are dealing with is the restoration of meaning and significance to all aspects of living and how writing works hand-in-glove with any concept of creation and any act of creation. If you make something, it will *matter* that you make it. There is always a sense of purpose, even if it is a desperate act forged from the heart of despair. Even if it doesn't turn out the way you intended.

The ways in which writing restores the world in its true colours extends far beyond the covers of this book. In the last chapter I talked of holding the world open. Perhaps we can now think of how language *prises* the world open, *eases* it wide, joins in the act of creation to make many things where there once was one. We can think of ourselves as insisting, demanding, seducing and encouraging this unfolding. This proliferation of fullness.

We can start with a single aspect of the world around us, or with language itself and a single word. It will soon become clear that there is a rapid to-and-fro movement outwards and back, from inside to outside, and that language is playing a vital role in the construction of both worlds. The inner and outer overlap to such an extent that at times it seems they are indistinguishable. At other times each is either the mirror-image of the other, or its protagonist in some way.

Let's look at the two possible routes we can take.

Firstly, the external world.

Today, I have a cold and am writing in the room where I normally sleep. In front of me, at the top of the bed, is a pillow. If I look at it and then look away, it is *merely* a pillow. It is so familiar that it is as though I discard it at once. But supposing I turn back to it and *ponder* on it. See where it takes me. The pillow-case is absurdly flounced, almost Victorian. Bought when I was in another house and creating a different flavour to the environment. So the idea springs up: my pillow was once in a different relationship to its surroundings. Which was also a reflection of the motivation of my mind in shaping the environment. (Who would

I be, in a Victorian bedroom? What in myself would be focused in that?)

Another direction: yesterday I laundered it in the local launderette. I count the pillow-cases as I put them in the dryer to make sure one isn't lost in the duvet cover or left behind in the spinner (my pink, beribboned pillow-case floating among a mass of socks and underpants, someone else's washload – metaphor for mingling?) There are three or four Scotsmen doing their laundry together. I remember how one of them....

So, my pillow-case has travelled and collected all manner of things; has gathered up the textures of life, environments, the outer skins of stories. As I write this, the pillow-case presses me with more of its storehouse of images and connections. And would therefore be the core of *my* writing-hour or morning, were I not bound to my task of telling you.

Secondly, the internal world. Close your eyes and think the word 'pillow'. Jostling, creeping around the edge of that word, a pillow edges in. A very old pillow, stained and yellowed, with a stiff striped ticking. I think of Grandfather's pyjamas and soft silk cord. Ironing them. Ironing handkerchiefs. We used to iron everything. The way the iron flattens out all the creases. (Metaphor: what irons out creases, pouring oil on troubled waters, calming? Muffling?)

You could continue, opening your eyes and scribbling briefly.

Back to the pillow. I feel irritation, immediately replace old striped ticking with white lace. Bridal pillow. Absurdly white. Mahogany. White lace and deep rich wood. Mahogany is one of the worst trees to cut, as it's old, slow-growing and would take centuries to replace. Love of it versus ecological conscience. Fathers and pillow-fights. Flying storms of feathers.

The pillows have multiplied; lateral movement, tracking outwards, sideways. Using the pillow 'out there' – particular, individual, with an unalterable shape, colour, texture. Yet stretched and changed by my associations. Using the *word* 'pillow', which then multiplies into many kinds of itself. And actions, events, moods, suggestions – all attach themselves rapidly to it. Once you are *open* to this process. Once *you* have opened the world to this activity.

I'll end with a statement that at first might sound over-the-top, but as one lives with it and as one explores, becomes a glorious reality:

Language multiplies the world (and ourselves) and joins with the play of the mind of God.

I dug this out of my notebook, written a long time back, and here I've brought it down to earth.

Like Prometheus. A piece of fire. Language a fiery chain.

Practice

Try out a number of journey-associations using both external objects and then the words for them, as starting-points.

Do this inside and outside of your house.

For example, today I might try four objects from this room I am sitting in now:

1) PILLOW   3) BEAR
2) TABLE   4) MIRROR

In each case, I will take an external route and then close my eyes and use the word alone as a place of beginning.

That's eight journeys.

Then I might do the same thing with those very objects but sitting somewhere in the open air.

That's 16 journeys.

Then I might walk to the park and choose:

1) CRUMPLED LEAF   3) SWING
2) PRAM   4) POND

I'll repeat the same process which is a further eight journeys, or 16 if you bring these four words indoors.

You may wish to try these at different points in the day, or do one each day for a while.

It's worth choosing a time-span since this creates pressure and boundary. If that helps. Depending on your mood, and how much time you have.

Or you may prefer to keep it open-ended.

But don't forget all the options.

Or that each 'structure' will produce new things for you.

12 GEOGRAPHY

> But most of all, it (saving the planet)
> involves the re-invention of what might be
> called geography, from *geo*, the word Socrates
> used for earth, and *graphos*, the word Plato
> used for writing.
>
> Tim Radford, Fears 3, *Earth*,
> *Guardian* supplement for Earth Summit, Rio, June 1992

I've always thought of Geography as a extremely dull subject. Looking back to schooldays, it was the option one tagged on at the end of one's choices as a kind of filler. If you were doing three arts-based subjects, then along with English and French or English and Music, Geography seemed a nice, neutral, safe option, blending usefully, bland and accommodating.

The idea that writing is always at least a two-track journey, both external (literal and geographical) and internal (imagined and invented) now becomes itself a shortfall. Looking a little further, we can see how in the practice of the last chapter, our external journey always has the play of the memory and imagination upon it, while our internal journey has the play of external reality (whether real or imagined).

We could therefore say that when we begin writing practice on a regular basis, we become aware that our own individual journey is always multi-faceted in this way. Also that embarking upon this journey – which is much expanded when writing begins and we are thus infinitely more *aware* of its conditions and meanings – we are travelling in the company of, or within, at least three universes: a) myself with my memory, expectation, recognition and invention; b) the world and its inter-connectedness, its associations, changes and qualities; c) the page, the life of language both to embrace all this and invent further universes that mingle, overlap and also draw you and your world ever further into them.

There is thus a continuous cross-reference and *fertility* going on between and beyond all these suggested locations. And what appears at first as a fixed and *locatable* spot (where we are or think we are at any given moment, where the world is or the page likewise) is in fact bristling with life and energy and is so anxious to be off, it moves as soon as we put eye, or pen, to it.

Geography means mapping. Writing within the realm of geography means making maps. Anything we write could be seen as a map and all our maps have a greater or lesser life-span, intrude a little or a long way into our landscapes; are more, or less, useful and enlightening.

A classic novel may have a life-span of centuries. My note about the particular colour of a flower may be as fleeting as that flower's own life.

Nevertheless both novel and note are interfering with the world, shifting it a little. Inviting either a single person who may be only oneself, or inviting the many thousands of people who read it across the generations, to come this way, look at it like this. To take on trust for a while and permit the temporary suspension of whatever may be one's 'normal' orientation and take up a new stance. For we look through a writer's eye as well as our own.

At one time, there were no maps. The earth was formless in this way – had no shape and extension. Then it began to have many maps and as we know, distance and size are relative.

If you think of Ordnance Survey maps, the same-sized piece of paper can cover a county or a square mile.

So writing scans and selects its boundaries and frames. Plays one against the other. And within the ecological debate lies the notion that the earth may need new writing, just as it needs the re-organization of its planters and husbanders.

Practice

Today I am woman coming to the edge of water
to wash linen caked with dust. How the air resists
my thighs, pushing through. How water clasps me
blue at the foot, white froth on my raking hand.

NJ, 'Opening the River', published in the collection *News From the Brighton Front*, Sinclair-Stevenson, 1993

1) Take a number of walks from your house to the water. The distance is a) 10 metres b) a mile.

   Use one sheet of A4 paper to write each journey.

   Pay attention to yourself and the earth, together.

Do the same again, but use:
a) half a page for the coverage of a mile
b) five pages for the coverage of 10 metres.

   Pay attention to yourself and the earth, together.

Note what happens in the working of each time-span/distance. Page and world.

13 HAND IN GLOVE

The image of a gloved hand is a potent one. I have hovering at the edge of my mind all kinds of unease, hints of silent intruders: the gloved hand that prevents fingerprints, the delicate, ultra-sensitive handling of things by the master-criminal for whom the glove is a second skin. Gloves as protection and prevention. Gloves worn for decorum. Or to emphasize the exaggerated outlines of a gauntlet, the challenge of committing the glove when the gauntlet is thrown down. That incredible sensation of wearing thin and skin-tight leather gloves that have to be peeled on and off like a stocking.

When I bought my father leather gloves for Christmas, the thrill of his hands inside them. As though I bought glove and hand together. Possibly the most intimate garment in its close-contouring of every surface, each digit of the hand. When we want to express an extreme closeness of association, a harmony of action so complete that the separate individuals are almost moving as one, we talk of them working 'hand-in-glove'. And a sense of secrecy as though such co-ordination were not of the common run, were almost subversive, slightly undercover. Like the hand itself, cased in its second skin.

We can think of language in this way, as close and familiar to us as a second skin. Speaking metaphorically, we can say that we work hand-in-glove with language in our probing and turning-over of the world. Like the most skilled handler of contraband or illicit and valuable merchandise, we are close in our collaboration with the words we use to best explore and lay bare the nature of our experience, our material, our ambience.

And we wear gloves for many purposes. To protect against cold or water. Or infection, in the case of doctor or surgeon. The glove is a symbol of our intimate association with language. It need not stand for language itself.

As soon as we think of a hand 'gloved', we think of it as qualified in some way. It is no longer *merely* a hand, an abstraction. Something that belongs to everyone, under the heading of parts of the body, not worthy of further notice. Gloved, it is a hand that has reached into the container, moved itself entirely to enter the second shape of itself. And whatever that glove is made of will be a material chosen for some purpose. The gloved hand is therefore already *mobile* and *purposeful.* If the glove is wool, it's more likely to be a practical intention that sent the hand inside. If fingerless, some greater dexterity needs to be preserved. Gardening gloves don't fit too well and are coarse and square. They stop thorns, nothing can penetrate them. Lace gloves show the skin through, and tantalize.

These thoughts grew out of a conversation I had one lunchtime with Graeme, who works for one of the larger finance companies and has helped advise me about a new mortgage. We were sitting in a small pub garden on a bench under a rose bush. I remember this because I anticipated an easy, rather lazy hour, maybe learning something about money markets.

What I got was as delightful and unexpected as the sudden combined burst of a wild rose tree and a long cool Kir upon the senses.

I had asked Graeme if his work involved psychological training, for the better understanding – and manipulation! – of his clients. He said he had learned to 'read' responses by the particular way a certain word is spoken. The word 'no' for example. He described to me how many different messages there were in the various deliveries of the word 'no', and how he could read an entire message from the context and tone of voice.

In this example, the word 'no' is qualified by all kinds of clues and associations from elsewhere. Meaning body language, facial expression, previous conversation.

But Graeme talked on, about how deceptive and how revealing language can be.

In Burma, he said, they don't have a word for 'hand', just by itself. There are many words for the different positions, attributes, qualities and actions of hand. So that contained in the one word is the-hand-and-something-else, much like the hand-in-glove. Already situated, mobile, conditioned. It's a strange thought, that there should be no word for the separate, solitary 'hand', as we have in English. *At root*, the world for the Burmese must be closer, more alive and vivid in its sensuality. The very language creates a more intimate and interactive engagement from the start. For us, we can think 'hand' and *then* what *about* hand? What is it doing, where is it placed, how old is it? and so forth. Technically, our language allows this moment of distancing, when the idea, or unqualified image, can be presented to us, even briefly, before its 'descent' into location. I could say progression/ascent/shift/drive or march into location. They'd all be interesting to consider. What kind of movement is it, in what direction, if I say 'hand' and then 'hand gnarled and crooked, rings biting into every finger'? The hand 'blossoms' into this extended image. Before this, it was – what? A suggestion, a shape.

But already I must protest. The 'it' that the hand was before it was a single-hand-in-particular can hardly be said to exist. So brief and so *purposeless* is the moment when hand is presented alone and unclothed by its place in things, we could say that it has no reality at all.

And so I come back to the same realization as before, that the word 'hand' is always used – whether voiced or written – within the 'home' or 'belonging' of its sentence. And within the space of the word and its collaborators (in this case, other words) – meaning the phrase or sentence within which it is presented – the activity of what shapes it is always present and working.

We are not so far from the Burmese after all. What is for them already contained in their numerous single hand-words, is for us immediately to hand (pardon the pun) in the rushing-in of detail. Whether such qualifiers gather round the naked hand and clothe it, or whether the hand produces such conditions out of itself – both are the result of our inability to live in anything but a personalized and located world. Even if, as I've said before, that world is composed of many overlapping hands, a fistful of gloves.

What cannot prevail is the deathly hand of no name which knows no touch, no work of time upon it, which floats like a disembodied spirit, a true exile. A state of mind in which a hand, or any other part of the body or the entire world *is* stripped of feature or meaning, must be acknowledged and recognized. We all have experience of it. If we're lucky, the experience is brief. But if this condition of things has such a grip upon a human mind, then the way back may be long and arduous. Writing can help.

Our language lets the poor thing back in. In this is our language a home, a country, an identity.

In this does it incarnate.

Practice

Two images to work with.

1) Firstly, we all know the chill and the horror of photographs of anonymous dead ones.
   a) Imagine such a photograph.
   b) Imagine enlarging it, focusing on the hand of one human being.
   c) Think of the Burmese words, when one single word stands for hand-and-something-else.
   d) Think of location, quality, movement.
   e) Make a list of location-hands (gesture, what is next to it and so forth).
   f) Then a list of hand-with-its-quality (colour, texture, shape, age and so on).
   g) And then hand-in-movement, perhaps thinking back beyond the death.

2) The second image comes from a book my daughter showed me. The picture is for healing purposes and is a diagram of the human body with limbs enlarged according to their importance to human functioning, including sensory as well as motor power. The hands were enormous, larger than anything else. Many times larger than the genitals!

   a) Spend a day, a week, studying hands. Decide upon a length of time depending on your circumstances. For example, it would be pretty useless for me to take a day on this. I've seen the butcher's hands today, and they were like sausages. That's all I got!

   b) See what hands are like in their quality. As explorers, communicators. In their texture and history.

Make your project to write the life of hands.

14 A WRITER PREPARES

Time is a splendid filter for our remembered feelings – besides, it is a great artist. It not only purifies, it also transmutes even painfully realistic memories into poetry.

To begin with the actor *is* not one or the other ... He may not have in his nature either the villainy of one character or the nobility of another. *But the seed of those qualities will be there*, because *we have in us the elements of all human characteristics*, good or bad.

Constantin Stanislavski, *An Actor Prepares*

I'd now like to turn to the idea of the writer as actor and to explore the 'as if' in its particular aspect of the creation of characters or first-person personae for you to invent, which are not yourself.

We've looked at the idea of putting voices into places where none existed before, and also at the suggestion to look at something *as if* you were in this place or that in relation to it. Or *as if* there were certain conditions, like weather or darkness.

Suppose we now look at writing an entire scene. We can consider two directions.

First of all, we may be wishing to recall and write something that actually happened. Let's take a family row, for example, at the dinner-table. Sunday lunch – father, mother and two children. Let's leave aside for the moment the argument that caused the table-cloth to be pulled – by accident or on purpose – and the china to crash to the floor. A moment of crisis and drama for all characters. You were present at such a scene.

Let's say that you are writing in the first person and therefore will be recalling *only* your own impressions and feelings at the time. Let's suppose you were the older child.

In this case to be an actor is relatively simple. You were *there*, and it is your feelings and perspectives alone which will need recalling. This involves the first layer or stage of preparation in which the ability to tune in to one's memories will be an essential skill for the writing of the scene.

Along with Stanislavski I'm calling this *emotion memory*. If we can reconnect to or call up the original emotion, we will have the necessary emotional charge to write the scene with passion and involvement. But more: if we are able to recall the original emotion so that it *moves* and *disturbs* us, it will carry with it a whole host of detail. We will *see* the mother's face, the dinner-service, the colours in the cloth.

If our intention is pre-chosen, then we will possibly not need to use numerous triggers for the *firing-up* of that feeling in its reality, upon which the writing will depend for its success. And by 'successful' I mean the valid, authentic emotional charge without which any amount of technical expertise will not redeem the scene and make it live for the reader.

This is the first example. Taking the same scene, let our second example be that yes, you were present and you have chosen to write a scene from your own memory. But this time you will take the position of the narrator. In which case you will be choosing all through the playing-out of the action how much of each of the four characters to present. Assuming the story is primarily about the older child – daughter or son – you may still wish to stay close to his or her reactions and observations so that the scene is played out through his or her eyes. Different collisions between him and father, mother and younger brother or sister.

Or you may wish to include the stronger presence of one other – father, for example, if he is the main protagonist. Or you may wish to include something from all of them in any case.

So here the emotion memory will need not only to work a little harder but also in a different way. As third-person narrator, you'll need to range further over the whole scene and all its elements, so that *the practice of using your memory* as something established in advance will be important preparation for such writing and can be employed independently of the writing and in conjunction with it.

Let's look at how your 'emotion memory' now needs to work differently. Your impressions within the actual time-span of the quarrel may have been limited and you may have to do some work of reconstruction if you are to write of the parents in a way that is emotionally real.

Now the suggestion that the writer needs also to be an actor can really prove its worth. You'll be asked now to do something that seems impossible: imagine what it would have felt like to be the father at the time. Don't forget that it is not the power of the actual memory alone that is at stake, but the *capacity to translate and transmute this on to the page.*

Here we are looking for the first time at the difference between writing out of your own direct experience alone, and the preparation involved in *constructing* and *presenting* a fully realized event – poem or fiction.

What would it have felt like to be the father at the time? You can work on two fronts: examine his state of mind, what is at play. Let's say you decide he feels threatened, cornered. Even though his attitude is one of attack. This involves an act of insight from you which doesn't merely assess the situation in terms of the most immediate evidence. He is enraged, but he has been attacked.

Now take your mind away from the scene itself and search through your own memory-bank for a time when you were angry but threatened. It may be that you were feeling this in the particular scene in question. But find other times, for this will be necessary work for when your scene is entirely invented. Allow the emotional reality that you will touch upon to conjure the context and circumstance. You'll be surprised at what you can remember. A moment of acute conflict – with a teacher at school? A lover? In the playground? In bed?

The second front here involves emotional empathy with the father. Take him out of that scene and put him into a scene where a similar battle is going on, and you are a witness, not a participant in the action. Align yourself with the father, see his point of view, *empathize*.

This double-front of emotion memory-use will serve you well. When you then go back to write the scene you may find your own inner emotional and memory landscape vastly expanded. The choices more readily available. You own *position* in the scene – whether first- or third-person, participant or narrator-onlooker – more charged and more fluid.

The writer is then an actor discovering and inventing himself. If for example you are required to bring alive a character who is at first sight alien to your experience, the previous angles and emotional directions will all play their part.

I'll give you three characters from my latest novel *Finding Him*: a wimpish university academic, a dumb village dwarf, a power-hungry farm manager who wishes to keep the village 'pure'. My lines of investigation were both internal and external and ran parallel. It was required of me both to use my entire experience of every university lecturer I'd come into contact with for the creation of Dr Nicholas Lamprey, as well as those I'd read about, heard about, seen on film. I'd take a movement here, a phrase there. But when it came to the emotional world of Lamprey, by which he lived and felt his way up out of the page, *then* I had to search for my own emotional equivalent and call up that seed or embryo, that tiny part of me that might *identify* with him if called into life inside me. So began an emotional search which took me deep into the heart of my own academic struggles and my moments of immersion in that, to the childish feelings that were operating hand-in-glove with the spurious adulthood of writing such disciplined (rigorous) material. And so by a curious transfer process did Lamprey come into being, having emotional injections for parts of him from parts of me – an irritating, manipulative verbal tactic pinched from the hated leader of my graduate seminar and so forth.

Archie, my dumb friend, had all my sympathy. I transferred his lack of speech to my own myopia and back, and identified with him in a basic frustration which went into different channels in each of us. I called on my own moments of being 'laid low', and the recall led me into an extraordinary and intense intimacy with the immediate environment. Close to the ground, to the nitty-gritty, so to speak.

And William Oakshott, leader of his pack, drove me into my own autocratic habits, troublesome to deal with. These drives displaced, transferred and used to *good* effect at last as a transfusion for Oakshott.

Parts of us are revealed, called up or invented to meet the demands of the work. So the work itself, in collaboration with the writer, comes to exist as *co-director* who will ask of us to try this or that role, location, pace, pitch, time-span, locomotion, movement, feeling: that is, to try out all the possibilities of being human in a moment of intense identity between you and your offspring.

Jesse Semper, one-time mariner, must walk like a sailor. I re-ran the Channel crossing, Newhaven to Dieppe. Felt the ship heave under me. Felt the act of balancing and the new relationship to water. I walk in my room, in my head. I call upon and call up a friend in Colne, ex-mariner, teller of tall stories.

I write to *move with* my characters as they unfold. Into their reaching-out for touch, into their evasions and for their own humanity, to be endowed by me.

It's like writing-alive the dead or dormant bits of people so that one is in the business of resurrection.

Invent a jungle and then explore it; the growth of our characters is an ongoing business, like our own moulding. We must be prepared to work on the hoof, for they don't come fully formed, rising like Venus from her shell. They have to be coaxed, stretched, activated into their natures at every turn. Like the actor, you can't afford a dead moment, for they depend on you just as deeply and constantly as an actor is depended on to hold the play alive right through to the end. Like an actor, I have to go that far – must step into his shoes and *be there.* Wherever Archie is, or Nicholas, or Doris Makepiece. I must be prepared to go with them and to whatever emotional depths they reach.

So do we also create ourselves and unleash that understanding and experience that the work enables us to gain.

The invitation here is to refuse the relative safety of becoming detached observers of our own lives. That is dead work, however polished and finely made. To take up instead the far more demanding but life-giving act of entry, empathy, identity. In this we always remain within ourselves, pushing back the frontiers of what we believed were the limits of our kingdom.

Practice

> Always and for ever, when you are on the stage you must play yourself. But it will be an infinite variety of combinations of objectives, and given circumstances which you have prepared for your part, and which have been *smelted in the furnace of your emotion memory.*
>
> Constantin Stanislavski, *An Actor Prepares*

I'd recommend reading the entire chapter on emotion memory in *An Actor Prepares*: Chapter 9, page 153 of the Penguin edition. Try out both remembered and invented scenes.

1) Remembered events.
   a) Make a list of some half-dozen events in your life when there was intense conflict.
   b) Choose three where you were involved and three where you were an observer or witness.
   c) Write each one in the first person and then as the third-person narrator.
   d) In each case concentrate on re-entering or calling up your emotional state at the time. As a reminder, you were possibly feeling a number of different things at once. Try out all the suggested routes:

    i)   your own perspective as participant/witness;

    ii) your own emotional reality as participant/witness;

    iii) as narrator, your own equivalent emotional situations for the emotions of the various characters taking part;

    iv) as narrator, your empathy with and understanding of the characters' points-of-view and emotional realities if feeling the same thing in a different situation where you are witness only.

2) Invented events.

    a) Choose some two or three scenes which are as far as possible removed from your own life-experience.

    b) Again, try out first-person identity with one of the characters.

    c) Then third-person narrator where you are free to select external/internal material concerning all of them.

    d) Work down a number of memory-tracks designed to lure or call out the relevant emotional condition from your own history.

    e) Work on all sources for external and internal characteristics using, as I did, direct experience, what you've heard from friends, read about or seen on film or TV.

    f) Plus what you can imagine without obvious and direct access.

Aside from the writing, practise emotion-memory as a regular discipline. Use a notebook to mark that you did this. This notation or reminder of memory could be used later as a trigger for more extended work on the page.

15 THE WILD CARD

... Now that my ladder's gone
I must lie down where all the ladders start
In the foul rag and bone shop of the heart.

W. B. Yeats

We're gonna rustle up some interference.

Humphrey Bogart

Once again, I'd like to persuade you into a process of un-learning. And again this means taking our inbuilt assumptions by the scruff of the neck and booting them out.

I'm thinking of our need for things to be complete, watertight, perfectly made. Images of supposed perfection offer themselves from screen, page and billboard. The perfect experience, life-style or product is what we are supposed to want, are seduced into believing we can have, should we buy or participate.

Some years ago, British Channel 4 Television ran a series of programmes with the overall single-word title *SOUL.* I have kept the accompanying booklet you could write in for at the time. In one programme, there was a contribution from the American mathematician Arnold Mandell. Talking about the strait-jacket of perfection in the area of theory or thesis, he told us that when he was a psychologist he was frequently required to throw away untidy or inconsistent data or information that didn't fit the theory he was arguing for or attempting to prove. Rather than *allow* a random and inconsistent element, therefore, *how things are* was sacrificed to the need for perfection and tidiness of the proposed theory.

I'm thinking how often we perform this act of closure or 'shrinkage' in our lives for the sake of a safe, definable and buttoned-up world. How we are less and less able or less encouraged to 'play' with the uncontrollable, that which defies a final definition. Useful to think back to Chapter 4 on utopias and the references to the language of fascism. The political or religious slogan is like the watertight theory – final, binding and *the last word*. Anything that exists outside it is dangerous, heretical, to be denied or destroyed.

On a purely personal level, one might imagine that in this we damage or restrict only our own psyche. But when the drive to limited definition becomes a collective act, we move towards genocide.

As a result of this interference with his work, Mandell moved from Psychology to Mathematics where he found more tolerant ground. The newly emerging chaos theory gave licence for a wider and more imaginative roaming of the mind within the mathematical field. Perhaps it is permissible for numbers to behave unexpectedly and thus defy control; not so humans. A day or so before I began this section, my sister sent me a card and note about a family matter. She'd attached a cutting, apparently by chance or perhaps as an afterthought. I was surprised and pleased at its relevance. It reads:

TODAY'S THOUGHT
Publishing a volume of verse is like dropping a rose petal down the Grand Canyon and waiting for the echo.
Don MARQUIS (1878–1937)

Don Marquis obviously died before chaos theory was born. But apart from the idea of intimate connectedness and influence between all things in creation, something as small and inconsequential as a rose petal can start a revolution in an individual or beyond, depending on the readiness of the receiver. I think Don Marquis was engaging in gentle irony here.

Yet to someone living 'poetically', collaborating with language, the gentle downward drift of a petal can be so significant in its beauty, it is *as if* a great thunder had occurred. I have known flowering bushes at dusk to blaze *as if* on fire.

That magical little phrase is our wild card here, the 'as if' that releases us from the literal into the metaphorical. The powerful little gateway that lets us out of our known and predictable realities where rose petals make no mark or sound, can only create echo. The ultimate authority on card games, a man called Hoyle, gives us this definition of the wild card: 'One that may be specified by the holder to be of any rank or suit'.

Within the bounds of the game, we have the widest choice of how to use this card.

The wild card, whether joker or one-eyed jack, is both an aspect of our imagination which we must allow as an element of the game, and is also the play of language itself upon us, *if we choose it to be so.*

There's all the difference in the world between a diffuse and drifting state of mind where we are entirely *at the mercy* of the arbitrary play of events upon us, and the decision to allow the joker his role *within the frame* of our chosen activity – in this case writing.

The joker breaks the rigid and predictable procedure of play and introduces a random element. The wild card's break-in *interferes* with the predictable forward flow of events. The wild card in this sense is writing itself, driven by imagination.

Persian carpets always contain a flaw in the making, design or weave. Some say this is the crack God needs to get into the world. A perfect and complete world is closed against all comers, it defies entry. As soon as there is error, a break with the perfect, then our interference becomes not only possible but necessary. For there where the pattern stops is disturbance, a buzz of difference and therefore the disconnection for the new dance to begin.

The crack, the place where the pattern breaks, that moment when what we anticipate is interrupted by the unexpected (unconformity) – there lies the source of new material, new openings.

Illness interferes with the movement of our life along well-known tracks. We are forced to re-examine, often re-organize our whole life. An illness can be a disease and traceable to a physical invasion, bacteria or virus. Or it can be a physical condition brought about by psychological causes. A *trauma* can assert its effects a long time after the event. What at the time was called the disease of 'shell-shock' was later rediagnosed as stress resulting from trauma. And trauma was recognized as not belonging only to the effects of war, but the assault upon a person of any intolerable violence.

Robert Bly in *Iron John* calls this 'the wound'. That which has wounded us often causes paralysis in a certain part of our being. Yet 'wound' in its psychological sense is where one makes the connection. Touches the heart of one's most fundamental life-experience.

Iron John received a great deal of attention in Britain both at the time of its publication and afterwards when groups began to form and test out Robert Bly's theories. Men withdrew from urban life for periods of time to engage in physical and emotional exploration, including ritual and drumming. The media coverage here was largely partial and distorting. I recall many an interviewer's opening remarks. You could hear the incredulity, scepticism, even mockery in the voice of a programme presenter, before the subject matter itself could be heard.

In this beautiful metaphor for non-utopian healing, Robert Bly speaks of the wound as a pool wherein you dip most carefully, going further each tine. 'Initiation, then, does not mean ascending above the wound, nor remaining numbly inside it; but the process lies in knowing how or when, in the presence of the mentor, to dip it in the water.'

We are not accustomed to think of grief or pain as anything other than shameful, that which must be buried. So the metaphor for recovery is that we go back underground, search out and become acquainted with our griefs, and touch the well-spring for new energy and creativity.

One of my deepest wounds has been the loss of unborn children. One loss in particular, a life that would have certainly formed into my last child, pressed so hard upon me that it was as if weeds were choking me at the root. I spoke to Malcolm Ritchie on the phone and he told me to let them live, let them out and talk to them. 'Speak to them, welcome them back in,' he said. And so I wrote *Catch* and 'caught hold' of my grief and gave it a shape and form. Netted my lost ones back in and gave them life on the page and gave their departure its worth.

I have known many men to have found this poem cathartic in their own mourning process being, as they are, less directly in touch with the loss of their child than the woman.

*

I've roamed around much like a wild card myself in this section, nudging at this or that idea, pulling the odd story out of the pack. I love packs of cards in any case, but I've also made my own. For a dozen years or more I've collected postcards of unusual and arresting images. Some are trick photographs, others collages. Some are photographs of paintings, etc.

I use them when running workshops, but they are also my own means of keeping alive the *wild card* in my writing life.

To deliberately maintain a random element, rather than simply hoping the 'random' will come upon me, I'll pick a card out blind and let it tease me into action.

The crucial word here is *response*. Out comes the card, OK I've seen it before. But now, today, what does it say, how does it speak to me and what is called out of hiding when I confront the imperative of answering what I've been able to give myself?

There's no escape. A cut tree. A grotesque china frog. Kids in an old pram, Byker, Newcastle. No way out.

The wild card lands and you have to play the hand.

Practice

Suggesting processes for randomness is a contradiction in terms. I can only point to tactics and methods for readiness. You'll have to trick and subvert yourself on this one.

1) Watching out for it.
   Spend a day, a week, focusing upon cracks, breaks in pattern, a missing house in a row of buildings. See how many *kinds* of sudden interruptions in pattern you can find. Write them in your notebook.

2) Write half a page of prose in which events logically follow one upon the other. Imagine something breaking into this orderly landscape. Try not to decide what it is to be in advance, but wait until you reach the point when you will let this happen.
   Do this each day for one week.

3) Begin to collect your own wild cards.
   You can also let your friends know you need strange and provocative images.

When you have a number of cards, say a dozen or more, you have a small pack and can begin working in several ways.

a) Deal yourself a card, face down. Decide upon a starting and finishing time. Turn it over and use the time in *response* to the card. Let it speak, let yourself speak in response. (Do not describe it.)

b) Deal yourself a card, face down, decide on a time limit as before.

When you turn it over, imagine the frame of the picture as a doorway into another world. Step into it and explore. Invent out of the beginnings that the card gives you.

c) Deal yourself one, two or three cards under the same time limits. What comes into play from the conjunction of images? What begins to happen as the images interact?

You can also work with friends or in a small group. In which case, deal cards to each other. If you have a pack of 20 you can place them down on top of each other one at a time and allow a few minutes for written response from the players.

16 QUANTUM AND SPROUTING BEANS

In the beginning was the Word, and the Word was with God and the Word was God... And the Word was made flesh, and dwelt among us...

The Gospel According to St John, AV

Jane has recently given birth to a son and is focusing on diet and nutrition. She tells me she's been reading a book about sprouting beans and how if you eat beans that have sprouted you are taking in the nutrition of a food that has an extra quality and energy. The sprouting bean has burst its skin and sent forth a shoot. It is in an active and energetic state and something of this quality is taken in when you eat the beans.

The bean is no longer a complete and self-contained item of food but is in a transitional state. You could say it is growing and you could also say it gives birth to a shoot out of itself.

It appears at first sight that the world is in a fixed and static condition. Like separate, distinct and unsprouted beans, the objects on my table have separate identities and can be named as such. I have a lamp, a bunch of dried flowers, a tray, a bowl, three apples, a book, a table-mat, reading-glasses, a New Testament, a tissue, a paperclip, five index-cards, my elbow. If I were with a young child, we might name all these objects to see how many names he can remember.

Like the child, in this moment of writing I perform a primitive act of identification. The objects so named are separate, closed in themselves. As such they are the first stage of an elaborate and infinite process of *identification* and *relationship.* In life and in writing, we'll move back and forth between the two, extracting and connecting.

The object in itself, within its simplest name, soon exhausts our attention. Indeed it *insists* on further investigation if we stay with it for any length of time. I begin to make a number of journeys whereby any one of the objects begins to extend its presence and its meaning.

This can be a movement out from the object itself into all kinds of associations, comparisons and connections. The bowl, for example, was a recent birthday present from a dear friend. It is very like the china you can buy at Charleston Farmhouse in Sussex, but she bought it in Covent Garden. I know this because I rang her this morning to ask. The colours are exquisite – peach and lilac. It is smaller than my usual bowls for holding fruit. It contains three apples. They've been there for days since my daughter won't eat the ones from the butcher that are grown on his allotment and I don't often eat fruit. I think I like the look of it too much, the colours in the bowl. So when I look and tell you what I see, there exists along with the bowl a hundred other things – memories, presences, tones, environments, a voice or two, the butcher, shopping habits and so on. These presences live and permeate the bowl so that it literally hums with the life it leads through me.

The bowl is extended. You could say it has sprouted like the bean, sending out shoots. You could say that as in quantum physics, this bowl is both *particle* – a separate, identifiable 'thing' – and *wave*, something on the move and overlapping with other realities. Present at the same time might be an image of Charleston Farmhouse, the butcher's beard, my daughter munching apples, the bowl that was here last week before this new one arrived. All these images or fragments of images merge and weave into each other like waves.

Here in words they exist in sequence on the page. But as I write and you read what I've written, the page-transmitter sends them forth again as co-existent. In fact my word investigation into this bowl has created the possibility and the reality of renewed simultaneous worlds.

As I write the word 'bowl', the object is present in all its quality for itself. It also shimmers and glows with the life passing through it, *relationship* called up by it. It is both particle and wave simultaneously, I can look at it in both aspects. My approach brings out one aspect or another.

In this sense, when we write, we are all co-authors of the world.

To take another route with the same idea: my bowl sits on the table with space around it. The objects nearest to it are the book and the paperclip. The bowl is a separate object and can have no possible identification with the separate objects of 'book' and 'paperclip'. Within the frame of my table, however, these three already begin to move closer in their growing association. The clip is yellow and there is *no* yellow in the glaze of the bowl. If I make the comparison, I make a connection that weighs in balance *difference* and *sameness*. And then the paperclip is there because it has held together the five index-cards which contain my notes for this chapter. The book is Danah Zohar's *The Quantum Self,* and my explorations concerning the bowl have been given extra excitement and dimension by her thinking.

So we have here the existence of separate particles but when placed within the larger system of my table and my project, each is connected to every other. In quantum theory, this is called *relational holism.* In writing for life, I call it a *poem* or a *fiction.*

Think of your piece of writing as a table on which you begin to gather a number of objects. The page becomes the frame of your project and within it, as they enter the frame, your particles also become relationships or waves.

As in the way we make sense of the world in that we ourselves cannot help framing it into clusters, so in the creative act of clustering language. And as with the dual nature of our objects, so with words themselves.

That original name seen as bean, or particle, soon sprouts or shifts into its wave-nature. 'Bowl' bursts its skin and becomes coloured; becomes gift, replacement, Charleston. And all the while retaining its identity as bowl. It mingles with the Bible, the paperclip, the tray, etc. within the larger idea of my word-movement here.

So you can let the page be your 'larger idea' and you can see how language repeats the quantum structure. You may write a single word and within the travel-span of the page, other words will collect as though to a magnet, having their own charge and combining with others to give off a different light and ambience.

We can extract things from the ever-buzzing field of our daily contact with the world. Only to return them to interaction, influence and relationship within their new setting.

It's possible to suggest that in our writing we repeat or echo the world's ambiguity, realize the possibility of simultaneous existences and so touch upon the mystery of Creation itself.

As people, we have all these aspects in our own natures and when we write, we perform that same miracle in our word-use. At once we are separate, joined, interfering, intruding, merging, overlapping, interacting.

As in our language, our poems and stories.

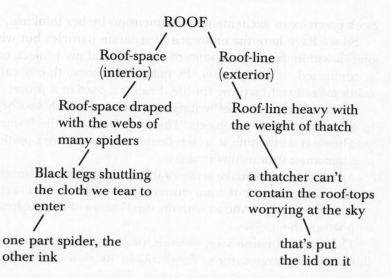

ROOF

Roof-space (interior)

Roof-line (exterior)

Roof-space draped with the webs of many spiders

Roof-line heavy with the weight of thatch

Black legs shuttling the cloth we tear to enter

a thatcher can't contain the roof-tops worrying at the sky

one part spider, the other ink

that's put the lid on it

Postscript

I am indebted to Danah Zohar and her work. Namely her book *The Quantum Self* and also her lecture for the Teilhard de Chardin Institute.

Practice

Travel the many possible routes I have outlined with any number of chosen or 'found' objects.

The routes are these:

1) After naming the object itself, an extension into its own qualities. Try not to stop at simple description but begin a process of association.

   For example, as with my bowl: lilac, like the tree in Grandmother's garden or the rinsed hair of my drama teacher.

2) An extension into associations not actually present.

   For example, where the object once was, how it arrived, previous moments of relationship to it. But allow these to arrive with you in a random fashion and with no necessary causal connection or logical sequence. Allow the images to gather, discover or invent the connections afterwards.

3) An extension into the immediate landscape of the object, relationship to objects near to it.

Become aware of two frames:

a) the spatial frame of your object – table, room, house. Or park, street, garden, etc.

b) the page's frame and what you decide (or what *is decided*) to gather there.

These two frames will be at once in harmony and in disjunction from each other.

Language and reality approach each other, pass each other, bump, brush against each other, spar and joust, or move in opposition. Like two people, meeting as friends, lovers, protagonists.

The tension of this approach/departure of page and life will add to the adventure and dynamic of your writing. Be vigilant for this. It will be an added power.

As ever, be sure to decide on a particular length of time for this 'Sprouting practice'.

You can try gathering your objects in advance for one week, one object for each day.

You could decide the starting time and then randomly choose an object at the beginning of the session.

You could use familiar and strange objects and also things found in the street or countryside.

Or one further suggestion: place a single object near your bed. When you wake in the morning, approach it and begin your relationship to it. Start as though for the first time each day. Don't read over what you've written until the end of the week. You'll be surprised at how this static thing has blossomed, revealed and moved itself through your pages. You'll also be surprised at the power of each day's renewal.

Try also playing with gathering by itself, using any flat surface. A table, or a cloth on the floor. Gather and dismantle as much as you like to get a sense of shifting and mobility. To do this separately from writing can create a loosening which is valuable for its own sake, and can also prime you for the writing practice which can happen elsewhere.

17 MIRRORS AND FRICTIONS

The 'bourgeois spirit' at every level of society consists in looking into the mirror, striking a pose to confirm one's social personality and thereby to keep what one has. Our aim, in front of that same mirror, is to obliterate ourselves daily in order to be reborn...

Jean-Louis Barrault, *Atlas*, December 1968
Quoted in *The Living Theatre*, Yale/Theatre, Vol. 2/1, Spring 1969

Writing reflects as a mirror does, but only partially. It also creates or constitutes a reality that diverges from our own in the inevitable selection, qualification and invention that we engage in whenever we write.

But there is more also: in writing we enact that important and necessary failure of direct and complete representation and at every turn call up the *friction* of language's dance and dialogue with reality. The way words graze as well as stroke the surface, the way they scrape as well as glide. Words can intersect the flow of time as an abrasion as much as they illuminate and reveal.

It is the lesson of separation and difference we must learn if we are to become fully grown humans on this planet. (And I don't mean our full measure of limb and height.)

This is echoed most acutely in our writing work. The language *refuses* to give us that rest and arrival. And in that very tension lies its power.

In 'The Wild Card' I touched upon the idea of language itself playing this trickster role. The joker who denies us that final and continuing identity with the other – which would in fact be death. There are temporary and fleeting correspondences happening all the time, of course. But until we are dead we must suffer this place of contradiction – where the writing takes us close, but finally throws back in our face and refuses us meeting-which-endures. Just as our becoming of the 'other' is, of necessity, a fleeting ecstasy, a place to visit, so also our language cannot actually *be* our life and loves.

This tension is the very source of our life. Will take us on to new books, to new experiences. To realize this is to embrace the very heart of *process*, that oscillation between 'the same' and 'the different' which is another seminal theme emerging through this book. And will recur for you as you take on this particular way of extending yourself.

Perhaps then the mirror of the page is more subtle than we thought and there is more than one function to its mirroring. Perhaps the words we put there will reflect and unlock our life – but the reflection will also be that of the approach, the near-miss and the thrill of the almost-met. That aggressive and passionate call to what is not ourselves, ringing back to us. The way it strikes against the world or the page, as a fist does. Or the cut of a knife-blade etching the name deep, making the sap run.

We can break the surface of things as much as we carefully peel back.

Another image that comes to mind is that of a jacket that won't quite do up. You can see the buttons and buttonholes, the body it must close over, and the cloth of each lapel stretching towards the other. You can see also how it might join and that it doesn't, and you can feel the measure of the gap in between.

It seems to me that when you take on writing, you deal with body, jacket, buttons and buttonholes and with what it means that there is that gap. Then you can play also with aggravation of this near-meeting, this space that will not close up.

Mirrors.
Narcissus, reflection in eyes.
Distorting mirrors in fairgrounds.
Continuous reflection syndrome.
Stepping through a mirror. Mirror with no reflection.
Women and mirrors, beauty in a mirror.
Mirror of the past, remembrance of earlier selves.
What the future might return from the mirror.
Walking through the mirror as a child.
The mirror's surface.
The mirror's viewpoint.
The wrong side of the face.

Practice

1) Raw material.

   Gather together all the ideas and associations you can about mirroring, reflecting and the opposite – what I've called *frictions.*

   This can be used as an ongoing storehouse of raw material for further writing.

2) Mirror-use.

   Approach your own face in the mirror once a day for one week. See how it is that your own face appears differently to you each time. What is it, then, that the mirror shows? More than just your image?

   Write about yourself as though the face in the mirror were that of a stranger to you.

3) Finished work.

   Complete a story or poem in which the idea of *mirror* and the idea of *friction* are both represented.

18 A DIALOGUE BETWEEN SOLITUDES

Love consists in this,
That two solitudes protect
And touch and greet each other.

Rainer Maria Rilke

The writer's dilemma and the human dilemma are much the same: how to satisfy two apparently conflicting necessities, the need for both individuality and for belonging.

I say 'apparently' since it would seem that these two needs are incompatible, that we must choose between them, go one way or another.

This dilemma is possibly more acute for the writer who lives out the contradiction most powerfully. He works for long periods in isolation yet potentially speaks to an almost unlimited number of his fellow human beings.

To encourage release from the stultifying pressure of this choice, I want to do two things: re-examine what we mean by *individuality* and *belonging* and also question the polarization that is set up by a particular interpretation of these ways of living which sends them into extremes.

We are persuaded to live our lives in distortions of these profound human concepts so that their proper meaning is obscured. *Individuality* and *belonging* become ideologies by which to live one's life, but in twisted and false form. Individuality has become the idea of a fortress-like entity, a selfish and in-turned pursuit of gain for one's own ends, an enterprise essentially in competition with everyone and everything around it. In this, the individual becomes *less* of himself, not more. In seeking to increase his separateness-*from*, he is diminished, entrenched and wastes all his energy maintaining this position for fear of destruction. Ironically his destruction is already well under way and intrinsic to this alienated and constricted state of mind.

To be an individual in this sense is to move in the opposite direction from touch, exploration and greeting and being separately alongside and connected.

Belonging also appears in its distorted form as we witness an increasing descent into nationalism, a blind and fearful allegiance to ever-diminishing categories of humans or group identities which inevitably leads to the appalling re-emergence on a massive scale of the compulsion to eliminate that which is unlike oneself – 'ethnic cleansing', neo-Nazi attacks on refugees in Germany and so forth.

In these interpretations, individuality and belonging are dangerous and damaging enterprises. The price of these allegiances can be war, whether between nations or individuals, and such attitudes are entering every sphere of our social, working and private lives.

While held up as beliefs and activities to aspire to, the sense of truth and validity in the ring of the words leads us forward – but into a trap. That is, we are trapped by a *definition of meaning* by which an original truth is closed down and replaced by a crude substitute. Once more, the slogan with its fixed and rigid contours has replaced the rich meaning and resonance of the original concept. And once more we are faced with the twin task of restoring the original and, strengthened in this, of finding a new way forward.

The man or woman who writes is doing business with these issues and cannot avoid the choice involved in being given the opportunity to initiate such restorations. He or she can return people to a more powerful and integrated sense of both individuality *and* belonging.

I have called this section 'A Dialogue Between Solitudes' in order to challenge the idea that solitude means isolation and an absence of belonging. In other words, to suggest a meaning and reality for solitude which dissolves the polarization we began with – that of individuality and belonging being separate and in opposition. We have seen how they are the same in their false aspects – the entrenchment which is inherent in both individual self-seeking and nationalism. Now it is possible to see that they can co-exist and be simultaneously realized if we look at solitude in another way altogether and as having a more generous and expanded meaning.

In our solitude as writers, we are aligning ourselves with all mankind as we pursue the project of expressing and externalizing how we relate to the world, what we find in it, how we see people interact, love, part company and manage their lives. How the world seems to me, how I would like it to be, how it could possibly be – all my simultaneous reflection and invention – when placed outside myself in the form of writing, becomes at once that which belongs to everyone.

So we 'belong' in both the ground we act and work from *and* in the end-product – in a restored sense of individual identity which is deeply interconnected with all others. I write of a man who cannot speak and so I write through him. In this I am identified with all forms of blockage to speaking.

We could then say that our solitude is a place of profound connection with all things. That in putting 'out there' some part of ourselves, there is dialogue already. That the world speaks back from what we, and *it*, have made together. The collaboration that writing always is, seems already to call into question the idea of solitude as being 'cut-off', a place of separation.

I see the page and its language as a two-way channel by which we send ourselves out.

By means of language which permeates and determines the entire world in ways I've only begun to explore, so does the world return to us likewise, along that same language-channel. The writer Alice Walker was so 'accompanied' by her characters when writing *The Colour Purple* that she moved her family – the family of her book – several times to accommodate their/her needs.

My friend and colleague Philip attends to the emerging souls who are his internal visitors and writes down what they tell him. At the same time he will welcome one more than another, and so she clarifies and defines herself and grows denser and more real as he watches and writes. And so she extends to him her company.

We can live closer to those at a great distance from us than the one who shares our house. We can at times be so utterly *alone* in the midst of our family group that it is akin to living in the heart of wilderness.

I mention all this to focus once more on the essentials of both individuality and belonging with which we began this questioning: we *realize* both at once when we meet, greet, connect and touch. I'd claim that in entering into such contacts with parts of ourselves and our own creations, we are also meeting and discovering the world and its populations: its stores, stories and its memory.

I remember again Paula Rego who paints so that she can see what's in her head; puts it 'out there' in front of her and so can meet and relate to it.

I remember also that marriage happens profoundly outside the marriage ceremony. That intimacy launches its laser across an impossible divide and that two lying side by side in the same bed for half a century can be enacting the most intense non-meeting.

Practice

Choose two solitudes to speak to:

1) Someone with whom you are intimate. In close touch.
2) Someone you don't know at all, a stranger, of no name who lives in another country or another part of yours. Name him or her.

Speak to each in turn. Concentrate on points of connection and points of distance between you, keeping in mind all the time the parallel dimensions of geography, gender, emotional and imaginative location, experience, condition of need, and the *solitude of the other.*

Note

The title of this section is taken from a discussion which took place at the Royal Geographical Society, London on 5 June 1992, organized by the ICA. I am indebted to Ariel Dorfman, Toni Morrison and Michael Ondaatje for their contributions and sharing of experience on that occasion which provided me with such added stimulus for this theme.

EPILOGUE

Whether or not you have read and explored all or only some of the previous 18 sections and their suggested practices, whatever you've gathered by now will be material for the next stage. It's rare for a writer to launch straight into a poem or story without some preliminary process – a flexing of limbs, an outline, a small pile of scraps. The possible forms that such process might take are so many and varied it would be absurd to try to list them. For there will be as many methods as there are people to try them, and you'll find whichever eccentric wanderings suit you best.

I hope by now you'll feel encouraged not to worry about making a mess, to be a little less weary or fearful of working in the dark, and that some of your preconceptions will have been overthrown or at least jostled sideways to make room for a host of possibilities.

So whatever you have gathered or gained, now may be a good time for a pause, an ordering, a review.

The triggers and stimulants I've offered here may have already led you off into more extended work. If not, you can approach your pile of pages in a number of ways.

Sort your writing into piles according to:

i) theme or content
ii) approach
iii) mood
iv) form, extended or fragmented writing
v) history

You may think of others, or prefer to mix them.

If you try out a number of different groupings, you'll first of all be sifting and turning your work over. Its very passage before your eyes may throw up strong conjunctions. You'll also find you may have, for example, a block of prose, a scattering of isolated words and a single vivid image – in one pile.

Whatever each pile yields, allow the elements of it (which are already your own) to turn in your mind and shape some kind of whole or extended piece of work.

If you are drawn to write a poem, extract those images and phrases which seem to you most vivid, potent and free from cliché. Try many different combinations and don't worry about logical connection. Put them together like a jigsaw or as though you were making a sculpture.

If you want to try a story, travel between the elements you

have made, using them like way-stones, landmarks or signposts. Don't feel obliged to use everything. Discard what seems to get in the way. But at the same time watch out for the power and function of that element which *doesn't* fit. This may give your writing its tension.

This is one method.

Another approach might be in the form of a lucky dip, or like sticking a pin in the map to create an arbitrary destination. Quite simply pull out one of your days' writing and without too much speculation, use it as your magnet or your starting-pistol. That is, either as a potency to gather things to it or as a launching-place out of which to explore.

Yet another approach might be to 'scan' what you have, and be vigilant for what offers itself as significant.

It might be nothing more world-shattering than the sharp presence of a commonplace object. A pen, a birdcage, a pair of lilac spectacles with a diamanté stone in each flying corner.

The poem will clothe your central image. You can begin by asking: what does it mean? Where is it placed?

The story will involve a more extensive unravelling. You may begin with the commonplace and then return to it, taking a haunting and curious route from start to finish.

You may enjoy the way various pieces of writing in your pile either dovetail, or suggest an abrasion or conflict.

Whichever way it takes you, you are now in possession of a considerable amount of source material, and armed with that achievement can go on to tackle and tease the world, your own imagination and language in endless three-way interplay.

PART II

Expansions

1 IN THE BEGINNING I: WE FED THE HEART

We had fed the heart on fantasies,
The heart's grown brutal from the fare;

W. B. Yeats

Why write at all, is the question you might want to ask. Is not the activity of dreaming, imagining or fantasizing just as effective? Is it not much more fluid, multi-dimensional and infinitely more far-reaching than the page could ever be? Why commit yourself to the apparent constraints of what appears to be an extremely small space in comparison to the limitless horizons and unchained movements of unbridled explorations in which the external record (or printing) plays a superfluous part?

At first sight and in the short term, we could agree with this. If the aim is to extend the activity of the imagination and so broaden the internal world, why apparently hinder this by the tiresome activity of getting words on to a page which within this viewpoint now seems like an interruption?

But wait. This is not at all as it seems.

The imagination, the ability to conjure, even if channelled or directed according to certain themes or key images, can only go so far. It isn't, however, a question of *replacing* this internal conjuring or dreaming with writing, but accepting from the start a collaboration between the two. Or to be more precise, a collaboration between many activities, the nature of which will emerge as you proceed and which I've introduced you to in Part I.

In the practice itself there will be many surprises, and all the suggestions and examples I may place here can only take you a certain distance along the way and can't by definition cover (and so limit) the discoveries that will arise for you personally.

Let us therefore look at the idea that the apparent confinement of the page might be a good thing, and what's more may in the end turn out to facilitate greater depths, new openings, a wider variety, a sharpened focus.

We all of us fantasize and it's probably true to say that a level of fantasy is operating in each one of us much of the time. Whether these fantasies are in the form of fragments, half-formed images drifting as by chance through our minds in situations where they have no obvious place, or whether they are the kind of fantasies that we deliberately choose to play out as a more or less complete and coherent scene, they none the less contain a number of worrying aspects. If defined as 'sufficient', then they may appear to serve a purpose or achieve certain ends. But in fact they may have little outcome other than a certain short-term release. They also have no *issue* or recognizable achievement or change as a result of their happening. Unchained one might be in wandering haphazardly in a dream landscape of one's own initiation, but this is so easily disguised as freedom. In fact the features and the emotional charge of the fantasy are more likely to be enslaving and constricting in their vague and diffuse outlines. One may well be locked into the treadmill of old and well-worn obsessions. The fantasy also is *safe*, in the way that for example a sexual fantasy may give you the satisfaction of total control, but eliminates that essential ingredient of all development and learning – the unknown quantity of another person. And in the case of the written, the unknown quantity of what words start doing and start throwing up (revealing) once they are actually *there*, outside oneself.

I have always found writing to be an encounter of the most tricky, exasperating and delicate nature! It can be compared to wrestling with an opponent, or the most delicious seduction of a lover. The comparisons with other activities are endless and these very comparisons are themselves enlightening and form part of the tools of the trade, as you will see.

The essential point here is the one with which we started: that there is all the difference in the world between a journey which is conceived only in the mind (of whatever nature and stature!) and one which takes place out on the page itself. And now we can turn the issue and look at it from the other way round and say that imaginative activity is 'confined' to the space of the mind only, and restricted thereby. I'd like you to think of the page not as a worrying (or even terrifying) blank and closed door, but as a place of wider freedom. The very opposite of what one might first be drawn to think. It might be a good idea to set out to prove this deliberately. Not to dismiss the guided fantasy as useless, limited and so taboo. The uses of such methods in meditating, centring, relaxing, changing one's mood, etc. are well known and well valued. No, the purpose of trying out the guided fantasy within the context of this book is to feel out for yourselves where the activity stops, where the limits of that activity are. And so to show you that we are engaged in a different kind of activity than that of simply transposing our internal meanderings on to the page. We are embarking upon an adventure which will start poking its nose into every area of life in a most practical and unexpected way.

To put it slightly differently, the internal meditation or imagining, left to itself, will, if successful, induce an easier state of mind, a charging of the batteries for re-entry into the activity of life.

Writing *can* change your mood and mind as an activity you take 'time out' to do, but can also in itself be an activity of life. Not a restoration in the organic sense alone but an extra limb. The use of which may add many worlds to your own and be a constant companion in all your doings. Or if you prefer, extend and multiply the possibilities of your own world to an astonishing degree.

So try the fantasy, and see its nature. You will find the edges of things slippery and hard to hold. You will find there are limitations to the span of your visualization. You might well be able to imagine yourself lying in a field in midsummer gazing up at the sky. Above you, a canopy of leaves is rustling and the light winks and flashes through the spaces between them as they shift in the slight breeze.

Even as I write this, I am working in two worlds at once. I put it this way for simplicity's sake. I am doing the exercise with you, closing my eyes and feeling the most pleasurable sensation. And at the same time writing down the *outlines* of that location, position of my body, what the leaves are doing, and so forth.

Now I ask the question: how much can you hold of this within your mind? Isn't it a question of the image or images being somewhat slippery customers, rather vague and always drifting out of sight? How long can you hold the scene in place and yourself within it?

To come out of this, you will discover that you have 'visited' briefly a place whose details escaped you, of limited perspective, somewhat blurred in outline. Nevertheless it gave you pleasure. It was relatively effortless to get there. Whereas I, in order to direct this, was wielding my pen and making the ink flow. I was working and using my body. I am also saying, fine. That was nice, that refreshes me. But what happens when you are bored with that? Do you visit another field, imagine a lover, imagine something altogether different?

Travelling in this way, across the surface, is one direction and one dimension only. Hard to catch, hard to hold. But does one 'hold' a thing more deeply, more closely, if one writes it down? I'd answer yes, and more besides. It isn't that 'writing it down' is simply to record an event, as a journal or diary entry might. If you read my short paragraph again, you could see it as a sketch, or a note, a reminder. These sketches and reminders can stay as they are or be the springboard for so much more. It is that 'more' which is the stuff of this book and this activity. If you write it, you have the possibility of finding out, of investigation.

I am asking you not to be peaceful (or only sometimes). I am inviting you to be discontented, inquisitive, bored perhaps with the easiest way and with the ready-made diary entry which merely copies the vaguest of outlines.

This is where the most essential difference arises between the fantasy that remains as such (that limited imagination confined to the head alone) or the active searching imagination brought into play on the page. This activity is virtually limitless in seeking or calling up distinctions, difficulties, struggles and efforts.

This is where we test ourselves and go further. Where the diary entry fails to provide, except to locate on a certain page at a certain time the trace of a possibility, and an invitation.

The diary entry, or the fantasy, may in fact be essential (though there are other ways to begin). But only as a door may be essential to enter a room. Or a foot to travel forwards along the path or ramble across uncharted heathland.

We are used to accepting these limited probings as our lot, and of thinking of them as the *end-product* rather than the bare bones which we then go on to flesh out. The destination rather than the very first step. Or even earlier, the flash of an image at the corner of your eye that sets the foot flexing itself, as though impatient to be off.

I hope that now your fantasies can be seen in a new light and that you will treat them differently.

Watch for the advantage. Rather than letting the flash of that skirt or shirt you wore when only thirteen come and go through your mind without so much as a trace – take control. Catch it as though you were netting a butterfly. Hold it close and see what it's made of. Like anything, it will contain many things for you, but not all the while it's flickering somewhere in the recesses of your mind and out of reach, with you a passive receptor of this and all other fleeting visitations.

Decide that you will *take notice* of these ghosts that make play with your interior world. And by 'take notice', I mean write them down.

If you buy a notebook for this purpose, you have already carved out a new space in your life for something new to happen. If you will allow these captured forms to sit there waiting for movement, you will have gone even further. They will bristle with invitation.

For me, this preliminary activity, simple though it is, has already moved me into a new relationship to things – an eagerness, a newly opened eye and ear. At the same time the ceaseless unchannelled activity of my own head is in a new relationship to me, and to the span of my day. I'd go as far as to say, my life.

I am already doing a number of things which can be seen as assertions, statements or questions. In this asserting and questioning, I become *active* rather than *passive* in relation to my own world. At the same time I open my life and shift its images from inconsequential phantoms to concrete provocative *meanings.*

For example, you might say: this skirt/shirt (this one in particular) that came into my head. And write it down. And now that I have written it, I notice something. It is not without colour, it is pink. You might then be led – and notice that phrase 'be led' – to 'notice' a number of things. Perhaps that pink is your favourite colour. That being so, you might look more closely and see that it is a powdery faded pink with an embossed surface to the cloth. Or that it sizzles like that pink of fluorescent socks and knickers back in...when was it? Or going back a few steps, pink is the least favourite colour, so why should I think of it? Ah yes, that woman across the street who shouts everything at the top of her voice, *she* wears it. But then, so did I – once.

We can see several things happening here. These activities contain both *assertion* (I will look more closely at this) and question (but *why* the pink, when I hate it? Or, *who* wore that?) Both lead to endless possibility and both bestow meaning and significance where it didn't exist before. You have selected and plucked something out from the random flow of things, and thus begun a journey *at an angle* to what would have been the direction of your life before.

You are in fact captured, as much as you yourself capture the object or event. The activity is two-way, with energy and meaning flashing back and forth between 'you' and 'pink skirt' much like an electric current.

Again I come back to the main point, that of the essential difference between this process 'remaining' (note the word!) internal, or letting it out into a space of great ambiguity. The space of the page both fixed and yet limitless. An interesting diversion? Or the potentially lethal extended awareness? Only by putting this activity out on the page can you hold its elements within the span of vision and so *ensure* the possibility of further adventuring. The difference between an idle and somewhat arbitrary imaging, and an active inventive process by which you become both author and spectator of your own initiations. It allows both roles and leaves the way open for many more. You will by now have a number of them under your belt, if you've begun at this book's beginning. What we are doing here is laying the foundation for literary production. Out of such capturing, examination and question, such messing about on the page, are poems and stories made.

You will already have begun to see the material of your own

life differently. You will have put that material and yourself into a new and more fluid relationship. You are now in a position to choose from a number of ways forward.

This skirt, I thought it was mine, perhaps it is stolen. What was the cloth like before it was this sizzling/faded pink?

Who was I with when the skirt tore?

It was under the pier. There were graffiti on the stone walls. Crude letters, red paint. Everything grey by contrast – sea, stones, pier-stakes.

These are my own imaginings and this is my *writing*. Don't forget that in the very reading of this book, you have your proof. For even as I write and suggest this or that opening, exit, way forward, I am forging it for you in the space that can be set up between us, passed between us like currency.

I have had this book *in mind* for a long time. It was not yet a book. And I needed to make it so.

I have chosen a pink skirt or shirt and written it. And *it* suggests certain assertions and questions *to me*. This is, at this stage, an example. Later, my 'example' will not be that at all, but my particular route to a poem, a story or an extension of myself out into my own created kingdom and my own previously dormant powers. Just as for you, whatever you choose will not be an example but the real thing.

This process I call the redemption of what is less or limited and its restoration is a force to take you much further than you already know.

This involves courage. It might take you to places of pain and difficulty. But it cannot fail to amaze you. Even in that troublesome area where pains and pleasures intermix and that upside-down world where doing business with pain, fear, grief can paradoxically lead to a gold-mine.

It is a brutal heart indeed, as Yeats said, and we all have one. A kind of brutality which erases that which might speak to us in its distinctive quality. Which might say, Oh that, that's *only* an old pink shirt. So desensitized can we become that all and everything is 'only' and so can be dismissed. Until we might dismiss our own very souls. This can become a form of collective and individual amnesia. When taken to extremes, a form of suicide.

Our writing invites the world back in, and our own selves with it. We therefore redeem and restore our own hearts, as well as all they may touch.

Practice

Preparation

a) Buy a notebook or notebooks. It's important to identify a place for the storing of your discoveries and what you will extract both from the world outside and the inner world of the imagination. Important also that you attach some significance to this notebook, that it has a certain value to you, so that there is a measure of importance to what you choose to hold on to.

From a certain point of view, we can think of our lives as a continuing exposure to random impressions from outside and fleeting impressions from inside – and both as arbitrary, fragmented or half-seen. Then the notebook becomes the place where such things are given a little more weight. Rather than passing through, scarcely noticed, they are invited to stay awhile. Perhaps to grow. Perhaps to take on a life of their own or be simply a small support in some other more pressing direction.

b) Decide upon time-spans, defined time and space, for writing in this book. For example:

i) Keep the notebook with you at all times and use it continuously, for one day, week or more.

ii) Decide upon a stretch of time each day. Perhaps half an hour each morning for one week. Or the same length of time each evening.

iii) Half-hours taken out of the day in a fairly random fashion. Four half-hours during one day only. More over a weekend.

iv) Give some thought to location. You could write in a favourite spot, or one you never use. You could write anywhere, wherever you happen to be, using time as your determining factor. Such as, five minutes on the hour every hour for one day. Or while walking/sitting in the pub/on a bus.

There is no magic to any of this. Creating a sense of pressure for yourself can produce surprising results. The very limitation can give rise to an unusual focus if you are 'jolted' out of your normal routes through the day. (Geographical, and how your mind usually works.) Even a sense of fear, irritation or tension can be the launching-pad for an image, an idea or a few words of no particular use at the time but to be stored and used later.

Remember the notebook is your storehouse, playground and place of discovery. It is the first stepping-stone. Here you are allowed to make a mess, dispense with grammar, allow things to rub shoulders or knock against each other that have never been placed in such proximity before.

The joy of this improvising lies in the very meeting of things that normally have no relation to each other at all in what we call the real world. Your notebook will become a place of movement. You could also consider it as a place of strange bedfellows!

Action

a) Practise an awareness of what passes through your mind, as though the random flow of internal shapes and forms were taking place on a screen and therefore slightly removed from you. This observation practice is well known for use in certain meditation techniques, but we are going further. Instead of observing this flow in order to leave it to wend its way through your mind dismissed and unused, interrupt it, intervene in it and select. Don't worry about the causes of your selecting this or that. Simply watch for what interests you, what it is that creates curiosity, attraction or even revulsion. Write down what you touch upon in there. Be accurate as to the detail.

For example, going back to my own choice in the chapter, I may catch sight of a pink cloth. If I hold on to this, I have more: a pink net petticoat. Taking this further, building the image, this then became 'the pink net petticoat awash through all its wires' – a line from one of my recent poems. Likening the stiff net of those huge under-garments we wore in the 1950s to 'wire' is a further practice we will come to later. For now, the task is to become accustomed to writing things down so that the habit is no longer strange and you pass through the self-consciousness, doubt (what is all this *for?*) and maybe strong reluctance that all writers must do business with at whatever stage of their practice.

When catching your images, write in fragments as sharply and vividly as you can. Dispense with sentences.

b) Practice external observation. Avoid sweeping and generalized impressions. Go for the tiny detail. This will be action that also precedes the decision to write it down.

For example, as I walk in the park I come upon fallen leaves. If I wait and reject the most obvious and the most easy note of 'fallen leaves', I can see that they are not all leaves at all. Among them lie scraps of paper. If I pick up one of the pieces I see that there was once writing there, but now only a series of blue smudges remains. And the edge is ragged, it was torn into pieces. So the mound of fallen leaves contains more than I thought. You will find that your first explorations on the page contain more than you thought if you will stop, wait and be curious.

This small example shows that the fallen leaves have become 'more' and have grown into a pile of fallen leaves and the torn scraps of a letter, smudged with blue.

You can see now that there are preliminaries to writing that have their place in other awareness-practice.

Following this particular procedure we are laying the foundations for an alteration in the way we see things. Not merely to observe what first strikes the eye, but to allow it to have a certain *hold* upon us, an invitation to see that things are a little more intricate than that. You will discover the richness that detail can bring and the way the world then becomes a place of specific and quite unique things that grow more and more like themselves alone and nothing else, the more we look. And language will come to our aid here also, as you will see.

At the end of your half-hour, series of half-hours or continuous week, you will have a collection of bits and pieces.

List them on a separate page.

If there are too many, make a number of lists. You will have created a landscape which is now independent of you and well furnished. You will also have gathered together a number of building-blocks for the foundations of poems or stories. At the same time and as an intrinsic part of the writing process, you will have moved the world and yourself together with the invitation laid ready to create entirely new shapes and groupings never before seen. Now you are in charge of new materials which you yourself have collected.

2 IN THE BEGINNING II: MOVING IT

Hamlet:	Do you see yonder cloud that's almost in shape of a camel?
Polonius:	By the mass, and 'tis like a camel, indeed.
Hamlet:	Methinks it is like a weasel.
Polonius:	It is backed like a weasel.
Hamlet:	Or like a whale?
Polonius:	Very like a whale.

Hamlet, Act III, Scene II

Now I shall introduce a contradiction. In the previous chapter, the intention and result of a greater focus on detail was to make the object *more like itself* and more uniquely itself.

Now we shall see that in comparing the object to another object or even an action, or to numerous other objects and actions, we appear to be moving outwards and away from it (so to speak) in a series of jumps into something else. Another landscape, tone or another 'container'. Paradoxically these departures from the object have quite the reverse effect than the one we might expect. By linking together our original point of focus and something possibly quite unlike it, we add fullness and richness to what we are looking at. Even if we link it to something close to itself in form or association, the effect is the same.

Whatever it is that is under scrutiny – in our mind's eye or literally there in front of us – is transformed in an instant. The object both *moves* as a result of our intervention and also bristles with possibility. It is no longer fixed and closed in its own skin as though that identity were a strait-jacket, but is let loose, as it were, to play with this or that new extended identity and emotional resonance. And in doing this we open up even more devices for exploring that object and increasing the sense of its own unique life, history and presence. History and association increase the sense of life. So does the world become more significant and meaningful to us and our readers.

We can see now that there is more than one way to make the world move and ourselves with it. You do not have to choose either yourself *or* the world in this act of changing – both come into play together.

Back to the pink net petticoat. Beginning the process of bringing it alive on the page (as opposed to the more limited life it may have if it remains in my imagination), I start to build on what I have captured. I can now write 'a pink net petticoat that looks like wire'. I have inserted the words 'that looks like' between the petticoat and the wire. I could have said 'that *feels* like', as though I were touching it, and we introduce the other senses into the arena. Using the medium of sight – but also touch, sound, smell and maybe even taste – the petticoat comes alive in a new way at each different approach.

The sample phrase which is your key to all this action, is therefore:

This ...... looks like ...... (eyes)
This ...... smells like ...... (nose)
This ...... sounds like ...... (ears)
This ...... tastes like ...... (tongue)
This ...... feels like ...... (skin-touch: hand, foot, cheek, etc.)

The possibilities open up thick and fast.

Firstly, what the petticoat looks like may be any of a whole range of physical objects: net, veil, grid. Or it could have a more fanciful association, such as, 'the sky after a couple of beers'. Meaning, what it looks like in the *mind's* eye. And then in this or that situation, or time of day. Or it could look like something from memory, a sudden bursting into the mind of a long-forgotten scene. The petticoat could become a cage, a labyrinth. In other words, a particular kind of place or space.

And so you can add to the implied question here: what does it look like *for you*? At once you are more active and more present, searching among the archives of your memory, your dreams, your life as it is now for the resonant place, person or event. Gathering up *more* to feed the image, once again the idea of expansion and growth appears, you and your images setting out on a parallel course.

The choice is always there: to look at the object literally, or to conjure and explore it in the mind's eye. The petticoat might then emerge in another place altogether: the Whisky-a-Go-Go Club, a basement café. Bare legs and high-heeled white shoes. How it looked to the people sitting on low benches. How it fell like a great puffball on to the bed. Petticoat into puffball, a visual and tactile comparison – but also more. A whole way of moving, seeming and feeling.

So you travel and like an actor pretend you are someone else with a different point of view – literally and metaphorically. A different sight-line, a different emotional charge.

To summarize: we have now isolated a series of simple questions to help the movement, which is arrived at by a more extended exploration of what's happening:

What does it look/smell/sound/taste/feel like?
What does it look/smell/sound/taste/feel like to me?
What does it remind me of?
What does it make me feel?

The petticoat looks like a grid of shocking pink. Delete the 'looks like', now that you've built the bridge. You now have:
the petticoat, a grid of shocking pink.

The petticoat is pushed to become something else, and the final result of this journey out and back is that it is both together. The simultaneous presence of a number of forms or angles is the miracle of word-use.

Collectively the questions bring into play *simultaneously* many dimensions of experience. They will call up past, present and future in the form of partial or complete memories, immediate or hidden associations in the present and anticipations of the future, real or imagined. And in saying this we are bringing together inner 'conjured' worlds and real 'outer' worlds. Do not worry if these intermingle in the same image or association in your writing. For whether writing or not, our lives are always composed of a rich soup of real and imagined material. We are inventing all the time. The questions insist also upon our sensual involvement. Real or imagined, your emotional links, your physical location (which will probably be a shifting thing) and your perhaps mischievous self might all wish to say not only 'What would it make me feel?' but also 'If I were my mother/father/lover, what would it make me feel?

These questions will serve to activate many parts of you so that the object or image itself is released into influence upon you. You will then begin to discover that something quite ordinary and banal is far more powerful and interesting than you had previously believed. And to underline the point again, change and movement occur in yourself and the object at once and increased meaning is accumulated where there was little or none before.

You might ask, what is the point of creating greater meaning for me in a single object? Meaning, I would suggest, is a means of empowerment. To value something is to value your own responses to it at the same time. If we take this process a little further, the cumulative effect will be to lead your life and yourself into a more fully active and interactive condition. This cannot but lead to a richer appreciation of world/self/page. And so to a greater perception and understanding. The internal and external world, intermixed as they are, become both more complex but also more subject to connections and management.

What may have been closed and blind or random and chaotic, becomes subject to opening and charting.

It may be worthwhile looking at what the 'present moment' has now become. It is no longer a discrete, separate thing, but the fullness of history and the potency of what is to come gathered in there as all-present in the here and now. Worthwhile also to consider this view as in opposition to fantasy where the present moment is *sacrificed* to either past or future and where the life lived becomes *at the mercy of* another time, an 'elsewhere'.

In our writing, we lay claim to, or claim back, ourselves. Call ourselves back into the present and all it can reveal. I have called this condition of openness,

THE EXTRAVAGANCE OF BEING THERE.

That we have more in us to use and manipulate than we are aware of. That any moment contains more than we think. That the world at large conspires to suppress and disguise this. That it can be a personal and political act to realize these things and resolve to do something about it.

In this we are seriously and playfully activating ourselves and the world within a dimension of time and space that is our right and our potential.

At first the idea of smell, sound, taste and touch may be strange to you as applied to certain objects. You may experience a feeling of foolishness, aversion, even disgust. This is because we are not conditioned to go very far in our relationships with the things of the world. 'Things' are often sold to us as a setting to aspire to, intricately bound up with esteem and our place in society. Media bombardment is predominantly visual and so overwhelming that there is little space for our own invention. Our other senses are rendered redundant.

The activities I'm proposing insist upon *space* above all. The opening up of space not available to you until now. Either due to the customary addictions to input, being 'fed' fairly constantly by the input of others. This comes mainly from television, videos, constant visual display which is 'extravagant' in one dimension only and requires only the briefest of attention spans. Little is asked of you and so little you will provide.

You might find it hard to write. But although gratification is delayed and of a different kind, you will discover increasing pleasure as the variety and power of your present-moments begin to increase along with your skill.

When you approach the petticoat with the aim of finding out what it smells like, you can play with the idea of a *literal* smell: roses (it's been sprinkled with perfume); cabbage (it fell into the compost heap); salt (it was discarded under the pier when your heel ripped the net). Or you can play with a non-literal image such as:

The petticoat smells like stale wine.

Meaning *not* that the petticoat has had wine spilled upon it, but that the petticoat *brings to mind* or *reminds you of* that morning after a party, a room full of bottles, fag-ends and a stale-wine smell in the air.

In these cases of less immediate and less literal association, a whole landscape may be called up and you can go even further in your chain of associations:

This petticoat smells like my mother's anger.
(*as if* you could smell it)

Sometimes sensations are so strong that they have the possibility of being more tangible than they actually could be or might be.

Imagine your mother coming in upon you trying on your petticoat, your secret purchase. She is shocked at what it has done to you, your transformation. (I'm using a scene from one of my novels here.) You could say: 'My mother's reaction was so strong I could almost smell her anger, a smell like a thick dark liquid, like tar or treacle that might threaten to engulf me.' I didn't write this, but it is one direction your writing could go in, if we take the petticoat as starting-point.

Here I have made links and so expanded into prose with the chain moving thus: petticoat-smell-anger-treacle or tar-engulfing. So that the connections happen almost simultaneously with the five links almost co-existing.

This is the magic of writing – its richness and density. Its many layers. For although in the writing I must lay out the elements along the line of the page, in my imagination and in yours as you read, they coalesce and make a moment's life which has many dimensions and experiences present at the same time.

Now let's try one more tactic. You can write:

The petticoat looks like a grid of shocking pink.

If you take out the linking words 'looks like' and write, 'The petticoat, a grid of shocking pink' then the petticoat leaps forward as that grid (or whatever). Thus the process we have used to make the connection, to conjure the association, need not remain displayed upon the page. Cut it out, and you have a more immediate evocation of the petticoat as something else and the slight distancing effect of 'looks like' is removed. You and your reader also enter further into the world you are making. The phrase or sentence is more economical, and you will see as we progress that such economy and density are more appropriate to the intensity of a poem. The unravelling and extension of language belong more to the writing of prose.

In the early stages of the writing process however (mine or yours), I find it more useful not to attach any particular practice or methods to a specifically desired result. And it is always the case that a poem may need expansion and prose can benefit from the sharpening effect of the pruned phrase or sentence. In writing practice it is best to play with images and words in every direction possible. To learn, first of all, what is possible and what can be gained.

I'll add one more possibility to our multiple list of approaches, 'as if':

It was as if my mother's anger smelled like tar, or treacle.
The petticoat rolled across the stones as if it were a puffball/as if driven by desire/as if I saw it on a film.
I saw the petticoat as if from the ground, billowing above my head like a forest of psychedelic leaves...

'It was as if' becomes the means of entry into the as yet unknown kingdoms you will discover and invent.

My dictionary says of metaphor: application of name or descriptive term to an object to which it is not literally applicable. I hope you will begin to see how to subvert and dismantle the 'literal' and so release the universe and yourself into your true natures.

To end this chapter, I'll answer two questions that may have crept (or burst!) into your minds.

You may ask, why do I keep to one chosen example and why a feminine one at that?

Firstly, whatever the chosen point of focus, to keep that consistently in view serves to highlight more clearly the range and variety of options open to you in relation to that focus. It strengthens the realization of the sheer extent of change which can arise from one single thing and your activity in relation to it.

As to its femininity, though I chose the example more or less at random, it crossed my mind that male associations may be as strong if not stronger than women's, and that men may well enjoy messing about with phantom petticoats from whatever angle!

A further question that might arise, is this: to those of you who feel yourselves further on and beyond such simple approaches, I'd say this. Although I've been writing for 25 years, it is still a surprise and delight (not to mention necessity) to begin at the beginning once again and see what can be unfolded from a pink petticoat. A net petticoat has served as a central image in at least one poem. It was the catalyst and springboard for an entire chapter of my novel *The Islanders* – though in that case black and orange with black satin ribbon and three tiers of net frill. The elastic breaks at the waist as a result of Caroline's sexual initiation under Shanklin Pier. The Teddy Boy (it was 1958) like a bird of prey, jacket flapping, tangled in her net. She returns to the dance-hall, her skirt unsupported, and it hangs limp and defeated and trails round her legs with too much length. The petticoat rolls like a puffball over the stones in a sharp, malicious little wind.

The single image proved to have much potential. You could say it served me well. But what is more to the point, in returning to that example again here in this chapter, I have made a number of excursions (in my example) which are routes not taken before, and I have that sense of surprise and opening in the writing of this that I hope you will find also wherever your practice takes you.

Practice

The twin themes of this chapter have been 'Metaphor' and 'Moving it', together with the deliberate identification and use of individual senses as *prime movers*.

Make a list of objects. You might like to do this two ways – firstly with ten objects in front of you, and then a further ten imagined objects.

In workshop situations, I have often brought to the session a number of objects deliberately chosen for their unusual or startling smell, sound, taste or texture (tactile quality). These have been placed in a bag and the bag is passed among the students. Each student will have his or her eyes closed, will 'explore' each object with each sense in turn. See which is the strongest sensation.

See also what is called to mind by the intense and isolated sensation when the visual is excluded.

You could do this with a friend, or in a small group, one providing unknown and unseen objects for the other.

If this is not possible, gather your objects the day before, so that they have at least a slight strangeness when you come to them fresh and without sight.

So let's imagine our lists with the senses in mind:

Present	*Imagined*
BRASS BELL	SUITCASE
FUR SPIDER	KEY-RING
PIECE OF CUT ROCK	PYJAMA BOTTOMS
FLOWER-HEAD	PAPIER-MÂCHÉ MASK
UNWASHED ITEM OF	BEER-MAT, STAINED
CLOTHING	AND BROKEN
PEAS IN A TIN	STICK OF ROCK
GINGER ROOT	POWDER COMPACT
SHOE	HAIR RIBBON
SEAWEED	MATCH-BOX (FULL)
OLD BOOK	BOX OF SOIL

Don't forget that touch means any part of your skin and the object will feel different according to the part of the body you touch it with.

Work through your objects.

Use the given sentences if it helps: 'This Brass Bell *looks/ smells/ sounds/ tastes/ feels* like…'

And then don't forget the more 'fanciful' association: 'This Brass Bell *seems to* (new comparison word)... ring with the sound of all the churches in Christendom...'

Or you can use the *as if* entry: 'It is *as if* this Brass Bell were ringing to remind me that not all bells are for the dead. This one sighs almost, a delicate brushing within its snake-embossed skirt...' And so forth.

Don't forget: *history, memory, elsewhere* (context), *weather, inside/outside, time-of-day, expectation.*

Don't forget: you can shift to a new *point of view.* Meaning: LOCATION – look from underneath *as if* you are a camera or simply look as if you are underneath; SOMEONE ELSE looking at it, *as if* you were a vicar, addict, child, father – and so on.

Or the object can leap at once into a *context.* My bell in a particular spot in the last house I lived in, or the day it was given to me. The fur spider a hideous tease by my younger brother.

Try also *cutting the bridge*: 'This brass bell looks like a dancer...' 'This brass bell like a dancer on her stage...' and you begin to make the lines of a poem. Or terse and vivid prose.

Key-words to Memorize the Process
METAPHOR
MOVING IT
SENSES
PRIME MOVERS
LIST – PRESENT
LIST – IMAGINED
LOOKS, SOUNDS, SMELLS, TASTES, FEELS LIKE
   (LITERAL, AS IF)
SEEMS TO
AS IF IT WERE
AS IF I WERE: LOCATION
AS IF I WERE: PERSONA
AS IF IT COULD, AS IF TO, ETC.
CONTEXT: PAST OR PRESENT
CUTTING THE BRIDGE

3 THE NUTSHELL

Oh God! I could be bounded in a nutshell, and count myself a king of infinite space, were it not that I have bad dreams.

Hamlet, Act II, Scene II

One does not become enlightened by imagining figures of light, but by making the darkness conscious.

C. G. Jung

Hamlet expresses a wish that all of us have – to be free of pain and difficulty and to be untroubled by bad dreams. He sees bad dreams as blocking the way to freedom and expansion, as though if they could be spirited away or banished, the smallest of habitats would stretch to infinity.

Most people will go to almost any lengths to avoid the pain-threshold, that place where our fear or sorrow is so acute it is as though we would drown in it. The more we take steps to avoid what we feel as the grip of pain – as though it descends upon us from the outside like the hand of punishment – the more does the unshed and unrealized emotion fossilize within. The more frantic our avoidance, the more this bedrock thickens until whole areas of our lives are as though petrified.

I like the dual meaning of 'petrified': to be turned to stone, to be terrified. Fear freezes, holds us back. Fear of our own pain is one of the most powerful preventers of growth and creativity. It cuts us off from our own areas of potency. We move within ever-narrowing parameters the more our pain-disposal mechanism displaces sources of trouble outside the area of use and process. Un*realized* trouble: source of wars, matricide, infanticide, rape, breakdown, revenge, excessive need for power, excessive claim to the truth.

There was a time in Western culture when the very purpose of art was to take the participant *through* such a pain-threshold. Greek tragedy had this function and 'participation' is the issue. One did not attend the play as a separate and passive spectator and only to be entertained. The play would touch upon the deepest human issues. Players and audience alike then collaborated in an emotional and spiritual journey which unlocked those feelings denied the means of expression, and *realization,* elsewhere. For me, a good book or a good poem or story serves the same purpose. Writer and reader travel together and unlock an experience or journey so that both are expanded. When I read a good novel I am in close collaboration with the writer as though it were my own life there, not someone else's.

I've just pulled out Issue Number 40 of *Book Case,* the W. H. Smith Guide to Good Books. It was free with the *Radio Times.* In there, I am encouraged to think of good books as a 'thumping good read'. I am told that popular literature has a very important place in most people's lives and the W. H. Smith Thumping Good Read Award is 'finally giving this type of fiction the recognition it deserves'.

This puzzles me. It's not popular fiction that has a hard time getting read. The promotion and marketing of such books as entertaining summer reading has always assured them of good sales and wide readership. Such books serve a specific function and we shouldn't pretend otherwise.

The experience of reading can indeed be limited. Here in the Guide I am encouraged to believe that 'good' means entering the lives of the rich and powerful and sharing their manipulations, affaires and fluctuating bank balances – as well as fluctuations in the sheer boredom of the prose. This is equivalent to spectator sport and spectator theatre, the ultimate form of the latter being the lavish musical. The essence of the experience is titillation, that you are transported by surface glitz and glamour to an 'elsewhere' of riches and nostalgia. Events and style have no relevance whatsoever to your own life. It is a case of the many watching the few, epitomized by the fervour of the reading public for royal scandal. We pour over intimate events in the lives of those who aspire to rule over us, and in the process we empty our own of significance.

I can hear the cries of 'élitist' ringing in my ears already! Not so, I am devoted to the popular. Only we need not to forget that what is supremely popular in our own culture has been chosen for us as such. A package of goods that it is in the interest of big business to persuade us we need. It is in their interests that we not think, question or touch the essence of our own condition. That we accept as most valuable that which demands *least* of us. That which is effortless.

'Popular' can mean something very different. 'Of' and 'for' the people is not always the lowest common denominator. In Italy today, every other village has its opera house. In Russia, hundreds of thousands of people turned out for the funeral of the poet Anna Ackmatova. Such writing was able to touch the heart of an entire people in its fearlessness in addressing their loss. While in Britain, practically the only poetry that squeezes into the best-seller list is the diversionary verse of a Wendy Cope.

For Hamlet, his bad dreams interfere with the small space of a nutshell's sufficiency and boundlessness. The bad dreams, he thinks, also prevent his *kingship*, mastery of one's own territory. The bad dream, you'd think, is the thorn in the side, the worm in the apple. If seen in this way, our bad dreams will seem to be poisoning us, *will* make us impotent. Unless we change our minds and think of all our dreaming, from joyous to nightmare, as a process of self-communication which we can harness for our greater freedom. Rather than endlessly wishing that we could get the whole thing safely packaged in something rather like a walnut shell. We say, 'to put it in a nutshell' when we want a complete summing-up and no loose ends. This may be a useful temporary device, but you're in dead trouble if you attempt to make your nutshell a suitable home.

As my father did.

In Clifton Road, Brighton, there is to this day a house called 'The Nutshell'. It was so named by my father when we 'went up in the world' and moved from working-class Bevendean to the Seven Dials – my parents were then 'in business'. The Nutshell was my father's statement to the world and himself that here was his kingdom, bounded and safe, all four of us packed neatly into the warm brown interior, not a nut to be cracked.

This entrenchment against the outside world was only a metaphor for a deeper confinement. The life of surface normality became even more grimly pursued the more it came under strain from the tidal wave of all our unspoken troubles. At all costs the image must be maintained. We were a normal, respectable, well turned-out family whose tracks through life followed well-worn grooves. My parents fought like crazy to shore it all up and paper over the cracks. But their own unresolved terrors and pains sped about the rooms like poltergeists as they acted out their games of power and subversion.

My father panicked when trying to park the car. My mother sat rigid in the seat alongside with a look of patient disdain. He couldn't get it right. And another day he would appear in his pyjamas and begin hoovering the hall when our neighbours were expected for dinner and my mother had the dining-table just so.

This tactical to-ing and fro-ing makes me laugh now, but at the time it caused their daughters to tremble in their separate designer bedrooms with no place to go.

And so we learned to be afraid of our own darkness the more they fought to avoid any acknowledgement of their own.

Pull your socks up, my father would say. And my wrinkle-free, upstanding and pure white knee-highs frayed as I tugged and tugged on them – tighter and taller they wouldn't go.

Never mind, my mother would say vacantly, watching out of the corner of her eye for his latest fall from grace. The demons spat and the ocean of their unconscious lives tossed them about to collide and scheme the other's downfall.

The house was full of spite and the unforgiven. Eventually, weary of its futile task, the watchdog in each turned full force on the threatening growth of children. I can remember The Nutshell bulging with the force of my need to *talk*. Like all of us, I discovered politics, sex and total confusion about why the world was the way it was – all at once. My inept and no doubt tactless approaches to my own and world problems at around thirteen produced a confrontation so acute that the blue-and-white striped Cornishware dinner-service still sails from the safety of its table to this day and crashes to the floor in slow motion.

Too much was outlawed and pressed to be admitted. As one of my poems puts it: 'We taste much later the belly of the sea'. It took more than a decade for that accumulation of unrealized desire, fantasy, expectation, loss, terror and unrequited love to be hauled up out of its hidden corners and resume its place in my emotional and imaginative landscape.

At the end of my novel *The Islanders* comes an image of resurrection and drowning for which I drew upon a recurring dream:

> I'd drawn up my drowned boy and he sits in the stern directing us across Monks Bay. Diving into the wreck, I'd found silver curls and I pushed Burnell back down among the rusty spits and worn planks of the splintered ship until he stopped breathing.

This image, which had begun life as a dream-fragment having all the horror and force of nightmare, was taken out of its dream-store to be given new form and purpose in the novel.

In saying this, I want to emphasize that the recording of dreams as a regular practice is only the first of many stages towards the use of dreams in one's writing. To begin writing as a life-enhancing and learning process, work has to be done either before or alongside work on the page.

If we think of dreams as one way in which we talk to ourselves and one way of bringing to light our own areas of anxiety, conflict, obsession – then remembering, recording and investigating our dreams can be a crucial part of that work. The dream 'talks' in multi-dimensional terms. It often lacks continuity. A single fragment can be so charged with meaning it is a source of exploration and unravelling for days. The dream can happen in a setting which is more than one place at once. Faces change, splinter, are more than one person at the same time. The Rock of Gibraltar sits in your living-room and the sea pours under the door. Everything is relative, all is up for grabs. And whatever part of ourselves performs this extraordinary feat of cinematographic brilliance, be sure there is a value in it. The nightmare you can't shake off will be a heightened and powerful eruption into consciousness of some half-realized truth. To treat it as your own gift to yourself, your personal private cinema, is already to cease cowering in a corner of yourself under the dream's weight of gloom. Right, you say. Let's see what's here, what's cooking or kicking.

I have never considered a dream in its entirety as material for a poem or story. Rather I will hold my dream-journal as valuable and sometimes sacred performance-space. And in using it, the very recording of my nightly jaunts will throw up themes, motifs and repetitions that find their way into poems and fiction simply by being *ready*. As in *The Islanders* with its tale of exorcism – the symbolic drowning of the dark figure of William Burnell who haunts and prevents Caroline's life – there will come a time when a long-past fragment comes into its own, is the right shape and presence to enter and illuminate my story.

For the shifting world of dreams is a useful model for our writing licence. Both dream and fictional space have that extraordinary quality in common – that of allowing simultaneous existence to things and realities, and allowing much more to come together in the same space than is apparent in normal waking hours. I found that in writing dreams down and using parts of them in the redemptive act of writing, they soon ceased to have the same power over me. It is the same for anything that arises from our own selves. If split off and its life denied by the freezing hand of fear or the indifference of suspicion, the area of pain will rattle in its distant underground hold like an earthquake tremor threatening from beneath, from the very ground we walk on. And driving us to ever greater camouflage and flight.

There is a half-way house between succumbing to pain and denying pain. Another place to go than the drowning of deepest anguish and fear or the brittle, entrenched ramrod of closure and banishing.

The writing-space may not offer consolation or reprieve and I do not mean to suggest it can replace the comfort of another human being's sharing, or redemptions of another kind. But in the end, and inside ourselves, we are alone with our pain. Writing can work with it, can translate and transform. It can also offer a landscape for the travelling of pain through us, a place to honour our griefs and fears and give them their entitlement.

But we love the ache, don't we? I asked a friend this question recently, trying to describe the way music acts upon us, that deepest sorrow when the fiddler shifts suddenly from a jig to a lament. The moment when a *source* is tapped, when it seems that what we touch is the well-spring of all feeling before it divides and forms into its particular locus and effect.

We can love and jostle, invite and urge our feelings through. When I lost what was to be my last unborn child, at least two years passed before I could create a coherent piece of writing to do justice to such a death. The poem 'Catch' does not approach the subject head-on, as do my journals and notebooks of the time. But the poem *does* lean upon the presence of those early, raw scraps. As though the event itself were at first too overwhelming for any kind of reconciliation; then filtered through by means of this object, that detail, until finally what had happened was *redeemed and resurrected in an entirely new form* through the poem's frame. And this is the way it works, that long-term, rich and painstaking act of digestion. A process whereby the material of pain is caught and used, partially and selectively, throughout one's writing-life. My troubled, unresolved relationship with my father emerging in another way, another form, in the tobacco-smell of her father's jacket as Caroline says her farewell on Shanklin Station (*The Islanders*). The rest of Tom, her father, is quite unlike my own real one. And my mute friend Archie in *Finding Him*, as dumb as my father once caused me to be, a single word choked deep in its burrow.

Or just to labour the point, that wretched nutshell popping up again in a poem early this year, *Reducing the Dose*:

> ... carrying me like a riddled stone
> to the water's edge; a brain, a walnut newly shelled,
> its surface cavernous and lodging in the shingle
> or any damned place where the world's blasphemy
> erupts into your ear and strangers offer up their
> gap-tooth smiles.

The penultimate line of this poem contains the word 'blasphemy' and this will mean something different to each of us. It may also be that the same expression will be blasphemous in one context and not another. *The Satanic Verses* is blasphemous to some Muslims and not to the author.

What is operating here is a threshold to the forbidden, a

dividing-line which if we cross we can be judged irretrievably damned, lost or forsaken. We all carry our own internal judge and the death sentence hangs over our heads if we are too crude, sexual, rampant, assertive, disrespectful, violent.

I'm thinking of blasphemy in its strict sense of utterance against the sacred, an act of profanity. But with this reminder: that we can imbue many things or aspects of things with sacredness – that which must remain inviolate.

The question then becomes, if we are 'profane' *on the page*, is this an incitement to excess and rule-breaking by others, or can it have another function altogether?

Let's reconnect with the idea that when we write, we do so for ourselves and also potentially for everyone. Whatever we write, even if it is done for a living, it is never certain at the time that what we create will make it into print.

When I make a poem or story, therefore, I am at root in business with myself, and only at the periphery of myself there may be a flickering sense of books, people, an 'other', a printed script.

Transgression has both religious and secular meaning: to sin or to step outside a given limit or law. As I write this, I become aware that I could describe my writing life in these terms, that it has been a continuous and recurring act of transgression – my own rules and those imposed on me, my own limits and those imposed on me. The writing then gives permission to others also to widen the canvas, to open even further the means of understanding and the field of recognition. To 'realize' ever more of what is possible.

It is important to know that the temporary suspension of all rules is a moment only in a wider process. Without the return to a wider but still bounded scenario, we will indeed plunge into excess and one that has no issue and no fruits.

There have been many times with writing students of unbridled licence, weeks of out-pouring, feverish overflow of excessive and uncensored imagination. The mind or vision roaming at will through fantasy, conjunction, flight.

This verbal flooding can be a time of enormous release and realization of power. What matters is that it has an end and an edge. But the marriage of such flow and subsequent selection and moulding (containment) is the most powerful combination I know.

As in life, so on the page. As in imagination, so on the page. It is as though both life and page provide – indeed *demand* – their own structure. Between, a brief and potent excursion into the unbounded. Somewhat like the parable of the Prodigal Son. The exodus and the return. Both equally necessary and to be repeated and balanced many times in the writing process.

In *Finding Him*, Al Barnes, one of my 'six stout men and true' who are the self-elected judges and punishers of the 'outsider' Joel, is haunted by a memory from his past. He once cut off the flower-head of his father's prize arum lily and was beaten for it. The guilt and pain fester in him and he is forever pursuing the enterprise of breaking and mending, often to the extent of trying to put things together that can't and won't belong.

This is not my own particular bad memory. But in writing out the scene where Alfred fails in his joining when trying to press upon Amy a doll which he had whittled out of wood, and trying at the same time to join himself to her as symbol of light and innocence – himself before he broke the cursèd flower – I achieved resolution for myself and my character at once. I travelled through his horror and pain, touching my own equivalent, and so knew it to the core.

This is just one example of the way writing allows enough time and space for knowing much later 'the belly of the sea'. Of dredging up that almost lost event and letting it loose.

Alfred Barnes exists in all of us. If I take him through the barrier, I realize an expansion in myself. We are intimately in step with what we create. If we track its movement carefully and with courage, we'll reap our rewards.

As they grew in stature within the story, my six stout men revealed to me many facets of human nature, obsessive, controlling, licentious. To give them substance, they needed more than a mere sketch. I had to live within each one, breathe each one's life, look from behind his eyes.

Practice

There are two strands to the writing-work arising from this chapter: 1) the dream-journal and 2) transgression (or blasphemy).

1) The dream-journal.
   Decide to record your dreams and keep a notebook by your bed. If you say you don't dream, having a notebook (container) ready will help you to remember. Soon there will emerge a series of recurring themes and images. Use these in other writing. They may well come to form the core images for poems or stories.

2) Transgression.
   a) Think of a terrible event in childhood when you were punished, banished, shamed.

      Create an adult character and a situation where that painful event is called to mind.
   b) Read the poem-sequence *News From the Front* by D. M. Thomas and Sylvia Kantaris. (This is reprinted in Sylvia's collection from Bloodaxe, *Dirty Washing.*)

      This is a sonnet-sequence, violent and sexual. In one of the stanzas, one of the protagonists utters a list of abusive names. This is a powerful chant-like verse which builds in power as the words pile on each other, the one more terrible than the last. We are taken through a threshold of the forbidden.

      Think of someone you hate.

      Write a poem-list, an accusation, a blame-poem.

      Use the most powerful images you can find.

      You could say, 'You toad, you runt, you seepage.' Or extend the images, as in:

   You toad, that sneers and slimes my stone,
   you wretch that tears my throat, that
   slithers in my groin to tickle at me
   pluck at my hairs, tear my sex out...

   (My examples, improvised on the spot, unedited....)

4 THE MOAT

As our use of language shrinks and as we pay less attention to the written word either as reader or writer, and in the name of efficiency resort to slogans for information, so do we collude in the expansion of dictatorship of all kinds. And writing becomes a diminishing faculty of discrimination and distinguishing. The unqualified headline can create a connection and plant a judgement in us almost without our knowing it.

A reminder of the dictionary definition of a metaphor: application of name or descriptive term to an object to which it is not literally applicable.

The use of metaphor is not always, by definition, a good thing and an expansion of possibility.

Again, language comes to my aid as a discriminatory tool and I can say, wait a minute – doesn't this depend on what associations you are creating and how much space or content is being allowed for that metaphor to be open to consideration?

An implicit comparing of one thing to another can be given (written) as an absolute, an imperative. Or it can be one among a series of comparisons, the purpose not the fixing and finalizing of an object or person within a certain frame of connection, but the opening-up of variables. The subject of the poem or writing then becomes itself *flexible perspectives*, with the object in hand an example of such application.

I'll give you several examples of the use of metaphor in which the connection made is the only one and the purpose indoctrination, the planting of a closed connection in the mind whereby there is no room for manoeuvre.

Firstly, a reminder of the use of film by the Nazi propaganda machine. The attributes of rats were transferred wholesale to the Jews and other 'alien' groups. No arguments were used, merely the punch and connection of various imageries and a handful of *core words*: rat, Jew, disease, Jew, plague, Jew, sewer, Jew, etc. If you are exposed to this at a time of profound social and/or personal insecurity, it is easy to lean on such absolutes and to take comfort from them as answers.

There is no room within this encounter with words and images for your own choice or meditation on the matter. Ambiguity – that most creative and flexible of conditions, that insurance of freedom – is ruled out of court.

So the fascist message and the fascist method are dovetailed. And since fear breaks man apart from his brother, so does a terrible distancing occur. The human beings with whom you have shared your life thus far – your neighbours, providers, fellow-citizens – are *translated* overnight into objects of contempt, derision, distaste and terror. A more recent example would be the 'ethnic cleansing' in the former Yugoslavia, which has torn that country apart, devastated the land and created for many thousands of people a condition of exile. The traumas of these events for individuals, their deeper stories, are now being written.

The detached observation of a fellow human being in this way is the first step on the road to his annihilation. Indeed, his humanity is already destroyed in advance of his death. It is cancelled in your perception of him as sub-human. And straightforward murder is as nothing compared to the torture and breaking of men and women that occurs all the time and everywhere throughout our world. This is not a matter of warfare between nations or groups whereby your enemy threatens you so you do your best to remove him, wipe him out. It goes further. In the end the Jews were wiped out in their millions, as were the millions of dissidents under Stalin. But not before they were reduced and starved and broken. And the trappings of their journey towards death – the normal, friendly stations, the orchestras playing in the death-camps – most powerfully embodied the hideousness of this stage-set for careful, calculated and scientific imposition of the means of disintegration.

Fascism is a death-in-life and behind it and hidden from view by the armies and insignia, by the *style* of the parade and public persona, lie *words*. (Or words that lie.) Simple words that cut off our fellow humans and *cancel within ourselves* the quality of humanity that connects us to all others.

At the time of the miners' strike, here in Britain, 1984, there arose a proliferation of words to cancel and reduce entire communities of men and women caught up in public struggle on the streets of our cities and towns. Yobbos, blacks, hooligans, thugs, scroungers, the underclass. Yuppies, hippies, ravers, skinheads. Hoards, mobs, masses.

Once we think of people in this way, our minds are open for immediate association with chaos, dirt, rampage, swarms, plagues. No one examines then the means by which we come to see in this way, nor the context and conditions which have underpinned the street violence or other conflicts.

The expansion of this subject properly belongs elsewhere. My reference to social and political events here is to remind us that attitudes are built up into edifices by the emotional charge of certain *words*. And used in isolation, in certain ways and with regard to particular associations, we can say that words can kill. And to repeat the point, words can lead to the extermination or murder of people, but also to the *death of their humanity and so of our own.*

This dehumanization has other less obviously menacing places of use and application. It is present in much contemporary, popular poetry. The indiscriminate use of metaphor for its own sake maintains a detached and voyeuristic stance across the work of many poets admired for their clever perceptual shifts, their intriguing angles. And there is somehow comfort to be gained from this particular metaphorical light falling upon domestic landscapes. Homeliness preserves the day in the face of brittle imagery. The trouble with domestic detail viewed in this particular metaphorical light which has no issue other than its own immediate sensation, is that the ironing-board may as well be the body of one's mother in the morgue or the dead children of Lebanon. There is no moral, emotional or value-conscious *discrimination* involved in the association.

I call this the dictatorship of the metaphor. The metaphor is uprooted, used in isolation for its own sake, does not support a greater understanding or vision. It does not allow the reader a landscape to explore and contribute to. Nor does it open up a territory within the poem whereby the reader can engage with movement and choice, with the question of doubt and exploration. Such writing forces a closed and fixed world, has all the answers and 'dictates' them as from above.

It is true that we need detachment to understand and to act with wisdom, but we also need the engagement of empathetic experience. We need to know when to identify as well as when to disown. And this can often be necessary with regard to a single event, or person. Words carry and create these possibilities and choices. We need words which don't pack home the authoritarianism of a single dimension. This disconnection from all but the immediate punch of the image – disconnection from human history and the wider landscape – can be fed to us in our fiction and poetry as much as in messages from those who would persuade us through the immediate propaganda channels.

It is possible for us also in our own writing to suffer from a kind of cerebral imprisonment which serves a political purpose. It directs attention away from the knowledge arising from the whole sentient person located in a sensual-political field. It is as though reality, with all its sensual and emotional facets, is slowly being translated into a glittering amusement arcade while the pier rots underneath.

This step backwards from confrontation or engagement with what it is to be human in all aspects, the sacrifice of depth to surface, will close off poetic as well as political possibility.

Language dictates or discriminates. We have the choice.

Two poets, each in the presence of his mother's dead body.
Here's Craig Raine in the mortuary:

> Like soft cheeses they bulge
> sideways on the marble slabs,
> ...
> two terra cotta nipples
> like patches from a cycle-kit.

'In the Mortuary', from Craig Raine's
A Martian Sends a Postcard Home

Here's Tony Harrison:

> It's on your warm palm now, your burnished ring!

I feel your ashes, head, arms, breasts, womb, legs,
sift through its circle slowly, like that thing
you used to let me watch to time the eggs.

'Timer', from Tony Harrison's
Selected Poems, King Penguin

The deeper we go into the particular, unique nature of an object, the less like anything else it becomes. If we pursue the same truth with our writing of human beings, it becomes impossible for the distancing and dangerous generalizations to enter.

It is in our hands, then, to keep in place this function of language as a barrier, an antidote to dictatorship. To hold alive an evolving, compassionate and empassioned world where domination and appropriation cannot happen, fed into, and led by our chosen words.

By way of word-use, the mind is trained or persuaded to develop the most sensitive and delicate of probes and will find another kind of security than that of arrival at the slogan.

Without such defences, a vacuum can arise in which it is only too easy for linguistic dictatorship to take its hold. For me, my writing has always been like this. A moat, you might say, to float upon or swim in. A medium of access that yet stands between me and the naked greed of propaganda. A moat where language sorts and sifts, twists in this more fluid medium and tests its chances. Or a garden in front of my house for cultivation, planting and flowering.

These are ways of seeing, or metaphors for what must be held alive internally. And the pages, the books, are my allies. They talk back to me and return to me the very fact that I will not swallow wholesale *how it is seen* by those who would cause our reduction. Or the reduction of any part of us, or any one of our number. I call my writing a continuous act of salvaging reality.

Practice

The work here is to see how the metaphor can dictate, or hold open.

Work through the following list more than once.

Firstly, choose words that reduce the life of the object or

person. Then work through again with an extended or open-ended and exploratory language.

His suitcase is heavy as (a) ...
{ Her tongue flicks in and out of her mouth like (a) ...
{ Her tongue is a ...
The sound of his voice is like ...
{ The humming of this stone is ...
{ This stone hums like ...
Her skirt hangs askew like ...
His silence is like ...
His footsteps follow her like ...
The horizon is like ...
{ The pier extends from the shore like ...
{ The pier is a ...
{ Sometimes love is like ...
{ Sometimes loving is ...

Loosen your mind. Turnover of images in your head/on the page, plus strong focus.

You can make such a list for yourself.

Make a list each day for a week and work through it with the idea of the image as *dictatorship* and the image as *suggestion*. Also an image of *cruelty* whereby he/she is *reduced*. And then one of generosity whereby he/she is given *fullness*. You could then play with a *generous cruelty* and a *reduced generosity*.

This work can be useful as:

i)   resonant starting-points;
ii) sharp indicators;
iii) movement creation.

PART III

From One to Another

Part III is for people in situations of particular difficulty or isolation. The ideas and realities explored here are, however, relevant to everyone, as I hope the rest of the book will be relevant to those who are more directly 'removed' from society.

In many ways such divisions are spurious. I work from the knowledge that confinement, isolation and disturbance are conditions we are all subject to at various times in our lives. I here speak to us all and to myself. But in particular to: those in hospital; children with learning difficulties; the bereaved; those with limited language-use; the elderly and very ill; those who've had a nervous breakdown; prisoners.

> We are both different
> And the same, and
> That is why we can
> Go round and round again.
>
> NJ

1 BUILDING BRIDGES

In the current debate, little is being heard from that submerged zone of our species, those who live far from the centres of power but are often near to the quick centre of suffering where ethical choices determine the immediate shape of things to come, and things to be postponed ...

I would also hope we would realize that what we feel when we watch and whisper and ache with these faraway people from faraway Chile could well be that strange trembling state of humanity we call recognition, a bridge across our divided globe.

Ariel Dorfman, Afterword to
Death and the Maiden

In this part of the book I'll be telling stories of how it is that bridges can be built by writing, by and for people who for one reason or another are in a situation of particular difficulty.

Here I'll be speaking to those who are more particularly distanced from activity, or what is thought of as valid activity, and speaking also to the people who care for them, educate them or guide them out of isolation or restriction.

I have talked in an earlier chapter about the role of the writer in giving a voice to people who are made mute by circumstance. The writer will then be someone speaking *for* someone else, acting on his or her behalf.

Now comes the work of teasing, inviting and encouraging voices into life from those who find speaking or writing difficult. Whose physical limitation perhaps carries with it a sense of limitation in all areas of potential *influence.* Those whose world and sense of self is badly shaken in some way. Or in contrast, those for whom the world is only too well established and rigidly in place. In either case, not much room for manoeuvre. As though a closing-down of so-called 'normal' channels for expression, movement and development must mean an overall cut-off.

In many cases it is the dictate of the *status quo* which

determines what is to be accepted as normal and the inability to comply consequently becomes 'abnormality'.

There are some communities – and I'm thinking particularly of villages based on the ideas of Rudolf Steiner – where distinctions between carers and cared-for can no longer hold. In such communities, difference and equality are in the right relationship to each other. Equality does not mean meeting some common criterion of good performance, or everyone trying to be the same as everyone else.

I'm thinking also of the extraordinary and rapid organization that takes place in hospital, when one's 'kingdom' is suddenly reduced to a bed and the ward becomes a village of inhabitants with various levels of ability. Collaborations and mutual exchanges happen right away. Visiting takes place between beds, those with their operation furthest away in time take on more responsibility – information, goods, comfort. Stories unfold, are repeated and elaborated. All are cared for equally by nurses and by each other.

Another image that comes to mind is of a Colombian tribe called the Kogi, subject of a documentary, *From the Heart of the World*, broadcast on British television at the end of 1990. The Kogi believe themselves to be the guardians of life on earth. There had never been any communication between this tribe and the outside world. Producer and writer Alan Areira made contact with the Kogi people through a go-between and had to wait a full year before he was summoned to a meeting. He had just that one chance to persuade the Elders to allow him to make a film about them and their lives.

The team ventured into the dangerous territories of Northern Colombia and were met by the Mamas (as the elders are called) at the entrance to a rope-bridge which swung high over a canyon and which we would need to cross to enter their domain. I remember this as a powerful metaphor of fragile yet robust communication. A rough gate opened, the narrow bridge swung ahead like a cord holding them to the outer world. The crew made their way along this precarious pathway towards the village at the far end.

We can think of writing in this way, as a bridge between

interior and exterior, between one and another. We can think of every human being on earth as a guardian, each one at the heart of the world and having command over a kingdom. A land which is both their own internal landscape and also whatever portion of the planet and its people they have access to. Managing and manipulating this territory is a responsibility we can accept or decline. It is our own to administer, and populate with all that we have ever known or dreamed, or may know or dream.

We are not used to thinking of ourselves as kings or managers in this way and of our own bodies and activities (of limb or imagination) as our own unique and special kingdom. It may at first feel arrogant or presumptuous to take this attitude, so we need practice also in allowing ourselves pride in what is ours to use. We are also well accustomed to being told what we are and ought to be. Whatever our condition, we can be encouraged to belong to ourselves, even if we are dependent upon others for many of our daily needs. There is in fact no one who is exempt from this dependency. The miners' strike of 1984 was based primarily on this knowledge and threatened destruction of relationship – that irrefutable knowing held in the bones, of the interdependence of each and every man upon the other, working underground.

As a writer, I try hard not to forget that everything I touch, use and consume is given to me out of others' effort. That there are hundreds of thousands of people who work to give me what I need.

No one is exempt. It is essential that every individual has the means to give what is theirs to give, and in many cases this can only be their own stories and experience.

Whatever the circumstance, the journey is always in the direction of getting back into yourself. Consolidation and valuing of who and where you are, rather than the reverse direction of 'getting out of it'. If you are hurt, confined or restricted in any way, it will be tempting to resort to avenues of escape, even if that escape is no liberation at all but a means of further enslavement.

Tempting for those in difficulty as well as those who care for them to accept immobility and ease its distress with an exclusive diet of drugs and television. Difficult to do otherwise in a country where resources for those who are ill or whose lives have in some way broken down, are ever-shrinking and along with this, the diminishing of growth on any level.

It is possible to act in ways that reverse this. There are pockets of time and space where 'walking in the chair' may be another option. By 'walking in the chair' I mean the internal journey that writing and imagining can offer. Writers who are entirely mobile do it all the time.

It is a waste of time to bang one's head against the inevitable, so we need to find another opening for movement and for our energy. Whether reading this, you are yourself 'stuck' and in need of movement. Or whether you are close to or caring for someone else who is, the writing examples and suggestions can be translated into your particular circumstances.

In the end, there is no special case. I'm hoping that all sections of this book will speak to wherever you are and that in starting to write you will weave a swinging rope-bridge so that we can hear about your interior – that precious contribution to the world's store of shared experience. I think of it as the earth's archive, with so much now at risk of disappearance. Not just the earth itself, but crucial parts of ourselves. And an archive needs contributions from all territories.

2 THE ERRANT BANANA

Some few years ago I was working on the W. H. Smith Poets-in-Schools scheme with a small group of what were then called 'educationally sub-normal children'. I believe they are now called children with special learning difficulties.

On the first two visits the poet works with the children and encourages their writing. The third visit takes place in the evening and consists of a gathering of students, parents and governors of the school for a presentation of the students' writing which will have been gathered into a photostatted or printed booklet, depending on resources.

The sense of self-worth gained by the children from seeing their work in print for the first time is invaluable.

After a period of time finding out about each child, we proceeded along a very bumpy road towards putting pen to paper. I gave the children one of my favourite suggestions: imagine you are a fruit or vegetable about to be eaten. At which point one of the girls giggled, shrieked and slid rapidly from her chair, establishing herself with her pencil and paper under the table. She stayed there for the rest of the session. I spent some of my time under the table with her. The idea had excited her so much that she felt safer, more contained in her house or shelter. I was pleased she let me come in with her and decided to discourage the two teachers present from their efforts to get her back on her chair.

But the crux of this group's dynamic came from another source. Malcolm was 16, unable to concentrate, restless and fidgety and constantly on the move. It was difficult containing him in any part of the room – until he began to write on the page. He was then remarkably still, though his body twitched and shifted along with the movement of his pencil.

He had chosen a banana, and without struggle he and his banana were one from the start. Under threat of consumption as it was, his banana went walkabout – diving down blouses, up skirts, flipping cloth aside, poking its nose into every nook and cranny, corners of rooms, items of clothing.

The result was a delightful piece of metaphorical foreplay. There was no overt sexual or anatomical language. The humour and inventiveness, the sense of freedom and autonomy in this piece of writing caused me great pleasure. Malcolm, I'd thought, might manage a sentence or two. As it was, the theme had triggered bottled-up, unexpressed force and movement and he'd danced his emerging and unrealized sexuality on to the page in a playful and thoroughly captivating adventure. What's more, when it came to the reading out of what each had written, the rest of the children shared an innocent and slightly 'naughty' delight.

It was my job to choose the work that would appear in the booklet and it was understood that I would be sent everything that was produced in the sessions. I'd wanted the briefest efforts to be included, since they can often be the least censored and most vivid.

When the work arrived in the post, Malcolm's poem was missing. I rang one of the teachers and she told me there had been some difficulty. I then got through to the Headmaster who had taken it upon himself to censor the work, *prior to my looking at it*, and had removed Malcolm's banana-poem for the sake of governors, parents and children, as well as the reputation of the school. I rang W. H. Smith's representative at the Poetry Society. The Headmaster's opinion must prevail. I thought of resigning. Of writing to the press. Then thought of the rest of the children. I wrote the strongest possible protest letter to the Head and to W. H. Smith Poets-in-Schools scheme.

Neither Malcolm nor his parents were present at the evening gathering. In my presentation speech I exercised my freedom and said how sorry I was that Malcolm was not present, we all missed him and were sorry his fine poem was not included in the book.

And so we moved to another poem, but a gentle wave of knowing laughter spread through the audience, who all appeared to have read the poem or heard of it and so were aware of the implications of its removal from the event. Malcolm was in fact more influential in his absence, and the poem's absence spoke volumes and was indeed a force to be reckoned with.

I was denied further access to the banana-poem and my request for a copy was turned down on the grounds that it was school property. Even though the work had been generated within the time and space of my responsibility and guidance.

I wish you could read it. A funny, inventive little poem, like many others, but for Malcolm and all who worked with him, a breakthrough.

I wrote and thanked him for giving us so much pleasure and for his valuable contribution.

I was not invited to tutor on the W. H. Smith scheme for some time.

Writing's deep trouble, you know. Once they get pen in hand you never know what they might get up to...

3 ALL THE LOST ONES

'Can't God find what he is looking for?' To this question Silesius replied, 'From eternity he is searching for what is lost, far from him, in time.'

John Berger, *Keeping a Rendezvous*

There are many losses, more than we immediately know. I have worked with people who have recently suffered the death of a partner, child, parent. Within the last decade, I have myself known the loss-by-death of Ernie my stepfather, my unborn child and Enid, a close friend who was almost sister. These losses are final and terrifying. They also gather into their frame many previous losses. Ernie's death brought me once more into close proximity with the dead form of my grandmother. My latest lost baby with previous miscarriages. Enid, my own age, pre-figured others' deaths and finally my own.

Thinking further on loss, we can see that death is only the beginning. There is loss-in-life. Of someone you are deeply attached to. The leaving of a marriage, the leaving-home of a daughter or son, a close friend moves away. And then the departure-in-life where the person goes nowhere at all but is quite simply estranged. Perhaps emotionally ill or distracted. An absence-in-presence which I have found as terrifying on occasion as actual departure. That distancing, that unreal quality in a relationship when you or the other is not hearing. Is elsewhere in mind or attention, fundamentally. The small loss of such times within a good and flourishing relationship.

D. M. Thomas' title to his book of poems, *Love and Other Deaths*. The terrible long-term loss of a parent you never had. A father or mother with whom you could never communicate, and which affects your relationships throughout your life. The retrospective loss of what you needed, what you *ached for* without knowing what it was, and never had. How you are hungry and search for it, perhaps without even knowing the source.

Loss of God, identity, meaning, dignity.

Loss of home, environment, possessions. Loss of history.

Those who preach that we should do without.

Those who don't take seriously the profound meaning that our possessions can have. That they feed and nourish in a way that has nothing to do with status.

The man who hangs up his suits in his cardboard house under a bridge in London.

Loss of memory. Loss of liberty.

Loss of the womb.

Loss of limb. The *active presence* of the lost part of you. That it aches. What is gone makes more noise than what is still with you, clamours for attention, nags at you for entry.

Loss of the *name*. Laura works with a man who has lost the names for things. He can't remember the name of his cup, his pyjamas, his hand. But he knows what it *does*. Can tell you its function, context, what it looks like. The hardcore is missing but interaction is intact. Laura works with the absent ones, helping to build bridges of another kind – between the name and the activity, its house.

She works to restore what is lost.

We can work with words, with writing, *towards* restoration. Even if we don't quite make it all the way.

Any experience of death involves loss of part of oneself. An obvious and somewhat unhelpful truism, perhaps. But hidden there is a further insight to be teased out. One cannot recover the lost beloved in reality, but one *can* recover many other things: the lost part of oneself that at first it feels they have taken away with them; the relationship itself, to be continued in a different form; the *experience* of loss, departure and absence must needs be given its due weight and value. Loss means less-than-whole. The bereaved feel a sense of exile as acute as a refugee. The mourner can feel as an exile in the heart of his own home and in the heart of himself.

Nothing can bring back the actual person who has died or departed, in their entirety. But it *is* possible to call oneself back to wholeness. The violent sense of being cheated or betrayed that a death can bring, is something to be worked with. Loss is protected by anger, revenge and righteous indignation. To call back the lost beloved and the full worth or meaning of their going is to allow the full emotional range and to allow all the conditions of our humanity to come into play. Then one regathers and touches the wholeness of oneself and the wholeness of events.

This takes courage. Writing can be a good companion in this. Danah Zohar (*The Quantum Self*) has spoken of wholeness as like a precious vessel which has been broken into thousands of pieces which are scattered across the world. To find wholeness again we must search in the world for the little golden shards and piece them all together. And so restore the vessel.

If we think of the event and ourselves as a shattered chalice, we can think also of the page as the place of its reconstruction.

Here are three aspects of recovery:

- of the lost part of oneself that one feels to have been stolen;
- of the relationship itself, transformed and continuing;
- of the full weight and stature of the experience, ongoing.

Robert Bly's book of male loss, *Iron John*, has produced exceptional polarizations. On the one hand from women and men alike who have poured torrents of scorn upon the idea of men grieving, discovering their rage and grief and attending weekend gatherings for exorcism. On the other hand, the formation of hundreds of gatherings, workshops and camps where men work together in an exploration and expression of their loss.

Not only do I find *Iron John* in its entirety a most healing and positive experience, but the reports of what is happening to men as they risk their gatherings, coincide with my own experience, for myself and with students, of the need to *get into relationship* with the father-who-never-was, the father-now-gone, and so on.

Men are encouraged to talk to the lost or terrifying father. I have suggested this as writing practice in the form of letters or written monologues where the writing itself has opened up the wound and led the student to the quick of the matter.

Write *to* him, in rage and longing.

Permit the conversations you never had.

Describe him in rage and in love to a trusted friend.

Imagine he is someone else's father and witness the struggle.

Finally, say goodbye. Bury him. Make a message for his resting-place. Make a shrine on a wall or in an alcove and renew your messages.

Beth's mother was always the opposite of what she seemed. Irritable, abrasive, nothing was enough for her. She expected, and got, service, attention, and gave grudging praise.

Beth was loaded with a sense of guilt. She told me of her mother's display – elaborate hairdo, flashy clothes, exquisite dinner-tables. The best in food, and no nourishment.

This is a mother never-present. Either when most needed, both in the early days and now, when Beth was herself crushed by the weight of all those years. Her mother recently collapsed and became truthfully what she had always been. A child, dependent, relying on everyone else for input and nurture.

The writing practice took a number of forms. As with men and their fathers, we worked on letters and monologues *to* her mother, *about* her mother. We worked visually and verbally. Beth drew some extraordinary pictures of her mother presiding over a dinner-table groaning with food and herself underneath it with the dog. Another drawing showed a baby with its feet cut off.

The drawings suggested writing-work. We took the following themes:

- Feet on the ground, absence of.
- Food, swallowing, nourishment.
- Display and what's underneath.
- Grotesque, monstrous, intolerable, (madness).

I suggested Beth re-establish contact with the ground. She began a course in the Feldenkrais movement method which explores the most primal movement of a baby, eg getting from lying down to sitting up. Time slows. You trace every movement, exploration and achievement of yourself as a baby. Beth's writing accompanied this and also went 'close to the ground', tracking the sensuous movement of the body – crawling, touching, licking – as a child might.

Improvisations on food and associations with particular foods. Beth wrote wonderful pieces on strawberries, avocados, onions, tomatoes. The starting-point of the particular vegetable or fruit led to memories, incidents or encounters she'd completely forgotten. 'Being stuffed' came into play as a theme. As did life under the table, metaphorically speaking.

I also encouraged the expression of her most violent feelings towards her mother. Using metaphor and simile, she built a monster in words, a grotesque and exaggerated mother nevertheless part of Beth's own experience. This 'figure' finally became so extreme, she was able to laugh as well as cry. And there was also some kind of release in proving that she'd done her mother no harm in this. The dispersal of that superstition we all have, that our thoughts can kill.

Go as far as it's possible to go, is what I always told Beth. Go to the ends of yourself on this.

The Fearful Image

In a writing workshop for the Arvon Foundation, I was using the card-pack, as described in Chapter 15, 'The Wild Card', in Part I. We were gathered round a table. I dealt a card to each person present, face down. I'd shuffled them beforehand, so I didn't know which card would go to which student. I indicated the start of a 20-minute session. Each student was to allow the image(s) to 'speak', to act as a trigger. I asked each student to be as responsive as possible and as open as possible to their own responses.

After about five minutes, one of the women, Sara, rose from her seat in considerable distress. She yelled out, 'I can't, I can't,' crashed her chair backwards and ran out of the room. Another student who had struck up a friendship with her followed her out.

Her card had come from the British Museum. It is a photograph of a body in a shallow grave or burial room, a few pots laid nearby. The body is not quite a skeleton, skin still stretches over the bones.

The card reads 'Model Burial of the Late Predynastic Period. The body is not mummified but desiccated by the hot dry sand which covered it.'

I discovered that Sara's mother had recently died and that Sara had been present at the death after her mother had endured a long, wasting illness. I experienced a few moments of guilt. Maybe one shouldn't 'risk' such strong images.

The first reaction of violent shock, horror and grief was, however, a necessary threshold. Sara had been keeping her emotions at bay and feeling particularly that a writing course was not the place for such overwhelming reactions. She therefore felt even more distressed to have been so exposed. But after careful and gentle exchanges and support from myself and some of the other students, Sara re-approached the image.

She took her time, spent brief periods in the company of the card, and in these limited stretches of time was able to unravel that devastating 'knot' of feeling which had sent her punch-drunk into flight.

The image drove her away and pulled her back. In her coming and going from it over the rest of the course she was able to assimilate and allow the flood and the awareness, able to begin to make a shape, an outline of her own within the landscapes the image had called up out of her. She was able to come near to death in all its power and complexity and to recover something of herself within that.

Her perception of the unknown dead person also changed, and therefore her mother's death with it. Beauty and tenderness entered in and weaved among the darker feelings.

Her comment on leaving was that she felt raw, wrecked but opened. Fuller, she said. She also had a few written pieces in her bag which were prints of her own journey through the card and towards her mother. Each person superimposed upon the other. As though time were cancelled and a ring of intimacy formed in Sara between herself, her mother and the sand-eroded stranger who unwittingly returned centuries later to send powerful influence into the bland morning light of a Devon farmhouse.

Crossings

When my stepfather's illness was discovered one late November and the news that he was unlikely to recover from the pneumonia which usually causes death in lung-cancer sufferers, I felt what I can only describe as a long silent cry of refusal rise up within me.

An echoing dark protest of such uncompromising strength, it was akin to a prayer.

Not yet, was its root. Just a little longer.

Perhaps the plea was for a reversal of the inevitable. Or a reprieve, and so time to say goodbye. The news was so sudden and unexpected. There was no time.

The energy of that resistance and longing was so strong that I called out to Ernie in his bed on the ward I was soon to visit:

> You rogue, you've cheated me by
> going off like that, out of our circle
> taking your war stories, your warm brown
> eye, the sidelong poke at laughter.

Ernie recovered from pneumonia and died a month later, in the New Year. We were granted a small licence, one extra month, a final Christmas.

Catch

Calling back, netting back in my lost children, gave them presence, gave a stature to my loss and guilt, established the events. Which before were drifting just out of sight, not quite realized. Haunting and flickering at the edge of consciousness like something you can't quite remember. And terrible anxiety somewhere, that you haven't yet dealt with it, caught up with the *realization.*

Writing – to realize. Make real.

I needed to acknowledge the brief unseen presence of these lives.

> ... so hearing that gathering population
> thunder in there, as though storm brooded
> way off over the Beacon where night is a little
> madder than I am, a little redder at the rim,
> I knew that my children call to me from their cells
> fisting for life, angry and dumb with their fish-mouths
> not to be carved by the good air into human.
>
> My eyes are fearful of these finished things
> clamouring their craft. I say to all my lost ones,
> love, hard to believe and harder still to catch
> allowed you out – too soon, too soon upon the
> world's clasp, you had no tools to swim with.

I say to them, I love you still my fish, my
                    unborn warriors.
                            Nicki Jackowska, 'Catch', from
                            News From the Brighton Front
                            (Sinclair-Stevenson, 1993)

Too Much of Ocean

Sometimes writing can catch the shadow of an event, the drift of it before it happens.

For a long time, a dozen years or so, Enid had been unwell in various ways. Each illness replaced the one before it and was equally serious and threatening.

One of her illnesses was water-on-the-brain. I forget the technical term. Using this as a metaphor, I wrote the poem 'Seahouse', reaching out for understanding of what was happening to her.

Enid recovered from this illness and it was several years later that she was diagnosed as having breast cancer. This was treated and halted but the illness recurred, this time in the lungs. She died at her home in Cornwall among her family, her husband and three small daughters.

Later I learned that Enid had been ever more reclusive and unable to pursue her own life and work in the years before her death. She was reluctant to spend long out-of-doors and stayed inside or close to the house. There was a funeral ceremony in her home before her body was transported to her original family in America for burial.

There were many contributions at the gathering, and John asked me to read 'Seahouse'.

It was as though I had known for a long time that Enid was inexorably moving towards death, had given up on life. And even some years before her final departure, had begun to move back, away from us and towards the sea. As though there was always too much water in her and the ocean pulling her, filling her slowly, her body-house awash ahead of time.

Her head turns blindly
towards its kingdom
fish-lights speckle her eyes.

Her skull aches with the weight
of ocean.
They'll need to drain her to
the sea-bed
for her breast-bone
the crusted fingers of her crab-life
where she sings rusty.

Nicki Jackowska, 'Seahouse', from
Gates to the City (Taxus, 1985)

4 THE POWER OF THE NAME

I grasped the two syllables closest to me, and replaced my
heartbeat with your name.

Anne Michaels, *Fugitive Pieces*

The terrible lightest wind in the world
Blows from word to word, from ear
To ear, from name to name ....

W. S. Graham, 'The Secret Name', from
Implements in Their Places

For those who are limited in vocal power, whether that be writing
or speaking, in using language there are two separate but
interconnected areas of breakthrough.

The first is the simple act of finding, inventing and uttering the
name of a thing.

The second moment proceeds from the first. Here is cat, cup,
man, *then* what is it or he all about? What can it do? What is its
life and meaning?

First language establishes identity, then relationship. The
relationship of the identified thing to yourself and to the world it
lives in.

This is a primary sequence for a child using language for the first time. It can be like this for me, in my beginnings. A single word or significant name will have enormous power and often the wonder of strangeness. At other times and later in life for a child, this is reversed and relationship is present as a primary event, eg hand-in-glove. It can work both ways.

Having devoted space to the use of metaphor and association, plus all its implied movement, I want to look at the act of naming in itself. How for many people in restricted situations, simply to name is an act of enormous power. For this is the greatest and furthest movement, that from the un-named to the named and the naming. A commitment, a choice and an act of precision.

For the man who has speech difficulties, to say one word may contain an entire landscape and its crossing. From the point of view of someone who has never written, the single word rings like a bell on the page – an arrival, a resonance. An echo of a life in motion and the trace of a claim on experience hitherto hidden and inarticulate.

If we think of a child, his need for a hold on the mother is paramount. Without that grip, the world is awash. The baby cries with total abandon, the fullest anguish. Slowly the learning happens and control is shifted from the all-embrace of the breast to another kind of taking-hold. Out of himself the child makes a sound that connects him to the world. The bridge of the single word uttered causes him profound joy. This shape on the page is in the most intimate relationship to that animal there. His mother writes the same name for the household cat. There is identity. It is the same moment of opening that adults experience throughout their lives, where there is correspondence.

It is said that the essential faculty which distinguishes us as human is our capacity to name. The man, woman or child who is impaired in the way of direct speech will enter their full humanity as the name is written, whether or not any more is undertaken. That single building-block, the power of the word, is the exercise of control, a lever on the boiling, buzzing confusion of a world otherwise without landmarks or stepping-stones.

Let's think of practical examples of how all of us use naming to prevent anxiety and to increase our sense of autonomy. In that narrowing of experience into a single name, we paradoxically create expansion for ourselves. As though we have stolen or borrowed a piece of the world.

We do this with our storing of photographs, keepsakes, gifts. Each thing plucked from the infinite mass of things is a bestowing of value, a holding back the flood of non-meaning.

In naming also, we choose this-in-particular, we extract it. Names proliferate in the public landscape. They are chalked on pavements, etched in tree trunks, traced in a window-mist, scratched in public toilets, daubed on advertisements, for sale in shop windows. These are the names of people, openings to universes of delight or pain. Calling back the lost, bringing nearer the distant. Conjuring.

If love strikes us dumb, then our joy in the name's mark must be akin to the realized intention of the written name by a man who cannot speak.

In my novel *Finding Him*, the mute dwarf Archie can sometimes make the shape of a single word. And having known moments when I also am struck dumb, I've traced the journey into utterance of Archie's single word from deepest undergrowth within him and in myself to its launch upon the back bar of the Cock Inn.

For Archie, to say one word is an act of devotion. He travels in himself and then out of himself, carried on the wings of his word to greet the one who has sent a message in his direction – a look, a wink, a greeting. Archie's word is supported by his dance – a curious hopping movement, an agitation of all of him, and the word, the core, the axis on which his body turns. Depending where you are, such naming can be a profound and earth-moving event. To write a name – your own, another's or the name of an object – is to claim relationship, insist upon it.

People can be transformed by a visit to their GP where their ailment is given a name. The nightmarish quality of a collection of symptoms, the way we work unconsciously upon those sensations and construct the possibility of serious threat. If we are told it is 'flu, migraine, then we are *located*. An unlocated source of distress nearly always multiplies in weight and significance until we are crushed beneath accumulated fears.

I had a student once who wrote a prose-poem which consisted

primarily of plant names. Their beauty delighted us, and also their slow parade as Philip read them out. Without further qualification, these names, some familiar, some strange, dropped into the air like stones into a pool and the ripples spread in us as though the intersection of that word and silence set up an agitation that would spread to who knows what horizon.

The biologist Miriam Rothschild naming the wild flowers she'd planted in her gardens to help preserve them against extinction: corncockle, cornflower, poppy, cow parsley. Carefully she cupped each one and named it and the sounds of the plants' identities called up layer upon layer of days and years in fields long gone.

Sometimes it is as though the plants are waiting for the name you give them, as though the world is reborn again each time you call it out. The world emerges, as it were, many times in your various and elaborate namings.

The single word can be a bridge between one person and another, between one person and the world.

This is like taking experience across a threshold and into a house where the shape of a single named object, placed as it is on the page, can begin to *act*. Language as threshold opening on to space lying alongside and also at an angle to our own. Intimately related.

A mere dozen words from a man whose life is poured therein has the size of a novel or a biography.

The name that distinguishes one thing from another, that makes distinct. If you are not flooded out by print as most of us are, imagine the impact. If I haven't had a letter for a week, a postcard with a single sentence resounds in my hallway like an orchestra.

To work with those who don't write easily is to remember the power and the sweetness of an early script. All parts of you gathered there as you grasp a piece of the world and the tremor of recognition.

The child writes 'bee' and the mystery begins.

5 RESISTANCE

... this is the most beautiful account I have read of age and ageing and the value you give to that. Lucie Cabrol gives us a new perspective on age ... and your story re-invests a life with beauty at the end of it. So we have a great sense of joy and opening out even in the body of the woman, and that helps to reverse the graph of decline which we assume for physical age.

Letter from NJ to John Berger, February 1983,
re 'The Three Lives of Lucie Cabrol',
from the novel *Pig Earth*

It is easy now to think of one's 'use' only in terms of productivity, ability to make money, to trade in goods, to engage in exchange of what can be weighed and measured. In cultures other than our own, the elders of the community are the guardians of history, the long-term witnesses of preservation and change which is a valuing in another time-space than that of immediate financial necessity.

After all, of what *use* is a writer, or writing? To entertain, yes, but many other things can do that. We need to ask ourselves, what is the particular value of writing that distinguishes it from any other activity?

In the writing-work I'm a step removed from instant material influence. This can so easily feel like withdrawal. But isn't.

To grow older is to face an inevitable restriction. A closure of movement in the immediate physical world. That writing is a movement and a value in another dimension is an idea to be kept alive constantly, whether that movement is a temporary alternative to physical mobility or a replacement for it.

No matter what your circumstances, to assert the value of your story is to resist the implicit dehumanization involved in investment and funding decisions which have a scale of values based on efficiency and measurable 'results'.

Just as I began this chapter, my daughter came home from her work in a local hospital which has recently opted out of Local

Health Authority control and become a self-governing Trust. I
listened in disbelief as she related to me the *transformation of
language* that is taking place where people are ill and ageing and
needing medical care.

Patients are called *consumers.*

Doctors provide *business* for hospitals.

Sponsors are *purchasers*, ie they are *buying* the viability of a
proposal concerning the treatment of sick people. This means
that there must be treatment for sick people which is not viable.
Money is present at every stage of the process. In this, the process
is transformed at the root.

The unit my daughter works in – understaffed, ill-equipped,
the garden too far away for it to be 'viable' to take patients to
where they might be renewed by growing things – must apply for
an 'Award' in order to continue.

The care of the elderly and sick must be argued for, financially
justified, must be 'won' in competition like a prize. It is no longer
a right. We are all in a courtroom, defending our need. There is a
worm at the heart of our social and cultural fabric and the
dimensions of our decay are breathtaking. I have written
elsewhere: 'Death, decay and poverty – material, cultural,
linguistic – are everywhere and spreading. The tools we use to see
and understand each other are as much under attack by the state
apparatus as are our health, education and social services.' ('The
Front Line', letter published in *Granta* 16, Summer 1985.)

The translation of human life into such terminology is a
violation of truth, a rape of our nature. We do not *consume* care,
nor *buy* it. This is a moral outrage. It can be fought in the public
sphere, on the political front, but it must be resisted at all levels.
And if you yourself are ill or ageing, then you can be active in
your resistance in another way.

Laura told me that the new language is seductive. If it becomes
common use, people will become accustomed to thinking in such
terms. She told me there are men crying on her ward and staff so
rushed they can only offer the minimum of attention, at times
merely for the patients' safety. She told me she had that day
experienced a collision of worlds so profound she didn't know if
she could continue on moral grounds.

It is possible for each one of us to act, whether we have the severity of a disease such as Aids or other forms of illness; if we are old and fragile and can't get very far. Each person, for themselves, can say: I have a life to offer and will trawl in my memory for contact and meaning and record it.

As one who is writing for my livelihood, I have myself needed to do this many times over in the face of the *defeat of value* which is happening across the world and in areas of publishing.

If you are old or terminally ill it is possible to look at writing as fulfilling a number of needs.

Firstly, time. We all know that inactivity is the problem of age and sickness. Time on your hands, doesn't time drag? Whatever movement is possible for you, I'm suggesting that writing-practice can enhance and give greater meaning to that movement, and extend its possibility.

What can you see and experience on the way to the corner-shop, the clinic, the next bed?

Secondly, the inactivity can be worked with if you become deeply engrossed in telling your stories – whether those are of past or present circumstances. Using the suggested practices, there will be a lifting of time's dead weight, letting the air in. A shift in yourself and what your landscape can offer. You can fill time with your own rich life, as well as enjoying the visual or aural results of others' imagination on TV or radio. However the world sees you, refuse to see yourself in such terms. Writing itself will help to create such resistance.

Perhaps it is possible to tell stories from every year of your long life. How it was. How it was for you. To trace the contours and bring out the texture of a time when the very material of daily life was different. How were your loves and hates? How did the streets and fields appear and disappear? The sheer magnitude of what you have lived through.

Perhaps it is possible to join with others in your ward, home or street for regular meetings, to read each other what you have written. And so together resist the decay in your perception of yourself that filters through the cracks and that many people working for you are also facing in their struggle to maintain the dignity of their work against a great tide of indifference, business-speak, the under-investment that is called rationalization.

Your immediate needs are probably met. You are sheltered, you have a bed, food, a radio, a television.

But there are further needs – to make a contribution, to speak. To reach out and touch.

Here's just one list of possible needs:

subsistence, food, warmth, etc.
protection, insurance in broadest terms
affection
understanding
participation
musing, reflecting
making
identity
freedom
communication

Writing can begin to fulfil at least some of these.

Writing is another *bridge* between one and another, and you need all the bridges you can find.

Our history dies with us. My stepfather died with many stories untold that I'd been longing to hear. Now my mother is unwell and a universe is threatened with extinction. I want the colour, sparkle, deepening and groaning of her age.

I think of a table worn with the many events it has hosted, the gatherings, burdens, battles, meetings that have happened across its surface, at its edges, underneath it. We all have our surfaces, borders, underworlds.

First, give your life back to yourself. The pages are infinitely receptive.

Then find a way, if you can, to give and take from another. Perhaps you can get help in this.

Queenspark Books, here in Brighton, have published the stories of those who would otherwise not be heard. And often the tale has been told by speaking into a tape-recorder and then typed later.

Your stories can light up what presses behind us, what came before. Can offer that altered state of mind that severe illness brings, inevitably a different relationship to the world, time and history. The kind of vision that perhaps only deprivation can bring. After an eye operation, the first blurred burst of a daffodil. If you can't see, the journey of a sound as it enters your space, and how the imagination flares at its touch.

Someone told me that the Royal Pavilion, Brighton, was used as an army hospital during the war.

You can attend to what is possible and fan it into life.

The story of the priest who was removed from his work with Aids victims since he insisted on touching them. The simple story of a touch.

Laura is closer to this form of deprivation than I am. As an occupational therapist, she knows the bodies of her patients closely and knows also each stretch to movement. She wrote:

> ...like a descendant from God, with your bushy eyes and mouth, I took you on a bus-ride. Like a green disciple I prepared my hands in a fashion to cup you if you fall. I prayed for you and shielded you from strangers. You rested when your knees were bending too far, you didn't want to kneel. Shaded glasses windscreened your eyes, keeping you at bay from me. So different from the cream-puff of hospital, the colour-coordinated staff outnumbering your presences. Cups of tea, routines, timings, acts, all contributing to the spongey, blood-sodden heartbeat. Medication in little plastic saucers. Patients throw back their vodka eager to be as drunk as everybody else, to please mummy.

4 June 1992

You will I hope gain personal pleasure and a feeling of growth and value if you begin to write your life. But there is more that your writing could do.

I have a suspicion, which is also a faith, that if stories were to begin to pour out of all the places where life is considered to be in suspension, or closing down, or without meaning or issue, the tidal wave might topple a few false gods.

6 UP THE CREEK

I've worked many times for the Arvon Foundation. For more than a decade I co-tutored residential courses for both Arvon centres in Devon and Yorkshire.

People book for these courses from all walks of life. The value of the experience, and my own approach to students, is that wherever each man or woman *is* when they arrive becomes our starting-place.

In the spring of 1986 I met John at the Yorkshire centre. He was a man of about forty-five and had very recently spent some time in a psychiatric unit recovering from a major breakdown. The sharing of such experience was one aspect of his need and this was already being met in support groups, men's groups, etc. in his home-town.

He had a further need, however, which is why he had come to Lumb Bank. He had booked for the course in some fear, believing (falsely) that he would be out on a limb, marked out by his 'extreme' circumstances. He soon discovered that a further half of the students had been through damaging traumatic experiences and were no strangers to medication, therapy and so forth. Those who hadn't had such direct experience soon discovered areas of their lives which corresponded in emotional experience and struggle. John's need was to go further than verbal sharing. He wanted to chart and map his journey out of illness and back into the world.

Arvon courses provide plenty of time for working on a one-to-one basis with students. John and I talked extensively about the closed world of hospital, the safety of it. The blandness of the environment. The way combined disturbance from many patients together in the same place can have a cumulative effect, and the empathy and collaboration among patients can mean a direct transmission from one to another of acute disturbance. This can spread like a current around the building.

John brought me pieces of writing which were realistic

accounts of ward life in all its clinical detail. I noticed that he was agitated as I read. I asked what was the matter. He told me he was dissatisfied with them. They didn't get to the heart of it. It was as though he were borrowing the language of psychiatric reporting and so repeating the journey he'd made, but not by way of himself. As though he were reporting his own life and it died beneath such a way of seeing and saying things. He was 'stuck' in the writing as he had once been 'stuck' in his darkness. I talked to him of metaphor. That perhaps he needed to translate the experience in some way. We were both working in the dark.

It emerged from our conversation that John needed to express and understand that there had been moments of clarity or drama, landmarks in what was for much of the time an instinctive and confusing battle. John was awash and then landed upon a moment of clarity – as though swimming from rock to rock, taking breath at each one.

I asked John to suspend all attempts at narrative, but to bring me a list of landmarks or stepping-stones, both events of significance in the life of the ward and moments of breakthrough and clarity within himself.

When we next met, he seemed easier. The list was a firm hold on a process otherwise too wide open. I then suggested that rather than try and *get it all in*, in a factual and sequential sense, he take each moment separately and fill it out, using the metaphorical 'nudge' of the questions I've mentioned elsewhere – what was it *like*, what did it *remind* you of?

Working on a few of these, his 'bald' moments began to grow and to become populated by those from within and outside the hospital. Chips in the radiator paint came into the scene. Fantasy-triggers and way-stones if you were trying to get a little further down the room each day. For a long time he hadn't been able to leave his bed. The day he'd travelled past a particular chip in the paint was a true achievement.

John loved walking and the natural world. As a relief from a static position and pushing therefore only inside his head to re-create the journey, I asked if he might enjoy doing this 'on-the-hoof' with physical movement driving the business on. It could be that he might re-experience *in his body* the stops and starts, tensions and easings that had marked his progress from bed to floor, and beyond.

He set out to walk from Lumb Bank to the village of Heptonstall. He came back dull and disappointed. Too bright, too many people, not a *route*, he said.

At the bottom of the valley is a river or stream. This runs past Lumb Bank which is built high up on the valley side. I asked him if he saw his recovery as an uphill journey, and then remembered how I had walked many times the twisting rock-strewn path at the side of the river, pushing upstream for my own quest in search of Orc. This writing/travelling became my odyssey for the penultimate chapter of *The Road to Orc*, a novel about the search for the ultimate wild, 'Orc' (Blake's unbridled adolescent) as the personification of untamed nature. (I remember Margaret Atwood's brilliant account of such a journey in her novel *Surfacing*.)

I told John about this and both books. We came to the moment's insight together – he would also work his way upstream, but in the opposite direction from myself *in terms of the experience*. That is, he would be moving upstream from chaos to order and resumption of control and autonomy. The loss and rediscovery of himself.

There wasn't much time. I suggested he map the route first, deciding quite firmly in advance his stepping-stones, places of beauty and resonance for him which would be where he would rest and face his moments of recovery.

I believe he did the journey three times, since we were by now near the end of the course and would go our separate ways the following morning.

There was a rising despair about not having enough time to make the trail, follow it again and again until the work was done. I told John, you can take it with you. The landscape of the stream and the ward are meshed inside you now. And then, one more safety-net: if you can't remember the exact location or exact features of one of your stepping-stones, you can create it for yourself. Find another place and superimpose it in the mind's eye.

John left with a pile of scribbled pages, a map and a purpose.

It was a potent story of catharsis – the relocation of a narrative, the opening of dimensions for the making of the journey, the provision of perceptual shifts and linguistic tools. I hope that John will go upriver many times. That he will continue to write from landmarks and outcrops, both in woods and fields and within his imagination. That the journey out of disorder has been so assisted by the charts and maps of writing that this will provide a sturdy wedge in the face of possible tremors and recollections in his future.

7 SERVING TIME

I haven't worked in a prison. Can only empathize with many ways in which people can become 'confined', locked up and isolated. I believe it is possible to transmute one's experience and so to touch, in some sense, the reality for men and women in prison. But this doesn't go far enough.

My colleague and friend Ken Smith spent three years as Writer-in-Residence at Wormwood Scrubs. He worked with lifers – men who had committed rape, murder. His experience and work is gathered in the book *Inside Time* (Mandarin).

Since this section of my book is written out of direct experience and up to now my own, I prefer to hand over to the first-person presence of Ken, and not attempt to imagine or reconstruct this particular reality.

The rest of this chapter consists of a letter Ken wrote me in answer to my request for a contribution to this book. The letter consists of Ken's own current thoughts and also quotes from *Inside Time*. I include the entire letter, virtually unedited. On reading Ken's extract I realized that what he is saying about men in prison and the writing process is the same as my own argument: *writing expands, releases, enlarges the possibilities for healing and understanding, wherever and whoever you are.*

Letter from Ken Smith, poet and Writer-in-Residence, Wormwood Scrubs, to Nicki Jackowska, 17 July 1992

Whatever I have to say on the subject is limited here to working with prisoners in a prison context, and they were all men; their isolation was obvious and demonstrable. Early on there's: 'I found there was no way I could talk about writing without working through the medium of a language of constant complaint and frequent hatred, where the verbs were threats and the moods sarcasm and longing and the adverbs probably insane.... so I let prison cast its shadow over every encounter, and took matters from there. Each prisoner must tell his tale in his own way, and poetry stirs the dreams and the ghosts.'

Later: 'The problem defined itself as trying to keep the imagination alive, where any stimulus to the starved prison self might be a starting-point, where language was always charged and meaningful, mercilessly so, and where men somehow survived to tell their tales, and where my task was to encourage them to talk, to write, to remember, to think, to keep the mind alive. Because I believe in growth, and the possibility of growth even amongst the damned, and because I believe that writing is a progression of thinking out loud, I therefore worked on the principle that the men I worked with were seeking help in figuring out who they were, their crimes, how they came here, and considered that they were in any case their own starting-points, and mine. Whoever they were, they knew things I didn't, and had no wish to know directly: the experience of having – many of them – committed violent crime; the experience of long imprisonment and the prospect of longer, perhaps indefinitely, till death.'

Paraphrased, that comes out as an affirmation of growth, and that growth comes out of thinking, using language to talk with or to write with. And by thinking I also include feeling. I came to realize that I wasn't just dealing with people trapped in isolation in prison: many were trapped in the isolation of being criminals, in a recidivist culture that repeats and repeats, with us as the victims. I'd say further, that it is people who aren't in touch with themselves who commit crime – certainly violent crime; they can't empathize, they're either macho or rebel or playing robbers with the cops or just hungry or just greedy or they've been buggered up somewhere, but they've cut off from feeling it (and I exclude the real sickos who enjoy inflicting it).[1] Creative activity, writing especially, because of the special qualities of language and meaning, leads to the feelings, the thinking it out. In practice I found those who used writing as evasion, escape, or because they wanted to swagger about and be a writer, so it has its dead side too – its failure rate. The rest of the book is disguised case studies, I think.

And anyway, it is communication, of meanings and feelings, and I think that has to be useful: the problem is the individual in there, trapped in whatever form imprisonment takes, isolated and lonely and unconnected. But only if they consent to; some I found happy enough with the well of silence all around them, though of course it's difficult to tell.

---

[1] See the opening paragraphs of Part II, Chapter 3, 'The Nutshell' for an exploration of the same idea.

PART IV

Samples

1 QUICK-REFERENCE WRITING-PRACTICE LISTS

List A: Beginnings, Turn-overs, Kick-starts

All these can be used as components for larger projects.

1) Themes. Using a theme as trigger; improvise, associate, make a page of jottings, eg as in List C.
2) Sound and Word. Sounds natural and mechanical. Find as many words as you can for natural sound, artificial sound. Listen to the sound of the words and if the word-sound echoes or opposes real sound.
3) Perspectives. Decide on a scene, several people in it. Imagine you are first one person, then another. Imagine you are fly-on-the-wall; spying through keyhole; close-up; long-shot. Try out short paragraphs from each position/person. Speak with that voice.
4) No-theme Automatic Writing. Ten minutes per day, same time each day. Don't read it over until one week has passed.
5) Alphabet Poems. Free-associate on each letter with qualifying phrase.
   eg A is for Auntie/I love to kiss, or
      F is for Frog/that creaks in my throat.
6) Twenty Questions. Create your own list of bizarre requests from simple to complex, eg 'What is the smell of rotten vegetables?', to, 'How does a worm turn?'
7) Association – Objects. Collect objects together on a tray. Pick out each one in turn. Give yourself only one or two minutes on each. Write everything that comes into your head. Work fast. Don't try to write sentences.
8) Emotion-Words. Hunting the concrete. Make a list, eg FEAR, DISGUST, JOY, RAGE, LOVE, FEAR. Write all that is for you associated with each word. Keep to one or two minutes for each. Don't use other emotion-words and avoid

generalizations. Find landscapes, fragments, things that are evoked by that feeling.

9) Senses: Distance to Close-up. Imagine approaching a building or person. What is it like: a) visually, what do you see? b) hearing, what do you hear? c) smell, what do you smell? d) touch, what is the texture when you touch?

10) Sounds, Progression of. Gentle and diffuse...to harsh and concrete.

   Make three lists: a) soft words; b) definite words; c) harsh words. Don't worry about the things but concentrate on the sound of the language.

11) Collage, Own Words. Without thinking, cover a sheet of paper with writing – images, impressions, single words. Cut it up and paste it up in different arrangements.

12) Slowing Down Time. Choose a coloured postcard. Write one short phrase on the back each day.

13) Inside/Outside. Spend five minutes in a room, write how it feels. Immediately after, go outside. Concentrate on the change, the difference.

14) Tarot Pack. Deal yourself cards in various ways. Allow each card to speak to where you are at the moment of receiving it. Let your writing be the voice of the card, or your response to it.

15) Free Association. Write any associations that come to mind with the following, giving a fixed time for each, eg three minutes:
   STONE, ROSE, BREAD, SEA, FIRE, BONE, HOUSE, STREAM, PUB, GRAVEYARD, RING, COMB, PURSE, THIMBLE, KEY, COIN, WATCH, RIBBON, KNIFE.

16) Metaphorical Forms. Take a word each day and work at it in all directions, eg SEA (Don't think too hard, loosen the mind):
   a) Darks of the sea, graves of the sea, dreams of the sea, gods of the sea, love of the sea, etc.
   b) Sea like blood, sea like the mind, sea like might, seaweed, seanight, seadead, etc.
   c) On STONE. lichen-covered, ragged, gorse-encrusted, foot-stepped, spat on by grandmother, etc.

Make up short poems after you've 'exercised' for a while.

17) Breaking the Mould I. A voice that would have: shattered the nerve of a dinosaur; coddled eggs; soured milk; brought my mother crazy from the bathroom, etc. Choose most *inappropriate* words.

18) Breaking the Mould II. Noun and adjective with opposite or antithetical implications, eg toothless attack; aggressive silence; the silk of barbed-wire.

19) Magpie. Make up packages of scraps. These can be like sculptures, eg one of mine is: two old photographs; torn handkerchief; lock of blonde hair; an old button; address card; chip of fool's gold. Use as needed.

20) Images in Opposition. Make lists of pairs of images in opposition, eg images of: stillness/motion, noisy/quiet, controlling/liberating, hard/soft, death/life, age/youth, confining/expanding.

21) Character, Viewpoint-shift. Choose a character not yourself. Paragraph each on: a) his thoughts; b) what's going on in the room outside him; c) move to third-person narrator, describe what he does.

22) One-man Consequences. Make lists of:
a) objects; b) qualities; c) verbs.
Connect them in as many ways as you can.

23) Theme Gathering. Keep an ongoing notebook in which you keep thought-provoking sentences. Here are some of mine:
In my father's house there are many mansions.
The time of his life.
In the morning they wore each other's face.
The mother-loving button-maker.
God has a migraine and dreams of snakes.
In the corner an old sailor is dreaming of tigers in red weather.
Our man on the spot.
Lost as if among the indian and the beast.
Soft as nuns and marzipan.

24) Metaphor. Compile instruction-list to practise use of metaphor, eg:
This purse is like...
This purse is ...

This purse hums in my hand like…
This purse…

25) Advanced Twenty Questions. Devise a list of quirky instructions which place you in unusual perspectives, eg Name three of your teeth. How is your luck? What lies at the centre of a marble? How far will you go? What is the sound of clothes coming off? What sound does a cathedral make? Describe the back of your neck.

26) Five Lies. Each day, choose five places, things, people. Lie about shape, size, colour, feel, smell, taste or function, eg 'The grass is fat as an elephant's foot.'

27) Corners: benign and evil corners. What is to be found in them? Metaphorical and real corners.

28) Cages. All kinds. From prison to your own room. Make it a week's project to hold this theme present.

29) Spells. 'One is for rain, two is for Spain, three is for water pouring down my mane.'
   Create spells, like chants or songs, to call up: a) weather; b) a particular desired event; c) a visit; d) a meeting; e) good luck.

30) You Are, He Is, Love Is. eg You are the sly dog/waiting outside the rabbit's burrow. Or: Love is the quiet sifting of one day's ashes.

You will soon become practised in devising your own short sessions. They will possibly become as familiar as daily physical exercise, so that you are agile with language and it becomes less intimidating to play with and use.

List B: Focus, Extensions, Meanders

1) Clothing. Choose an item of clothing, owned or desired. Write its journey: its making, its history. Write with the voice of the clothing. Protest, enjoy.

2) Music. Immerse yourself in chosen music. Immediately after listening, see how you write from the mood it has created in you.

3) Blind Man's Buff. Work with a friend or alone. Close your eyes, allow yourself to be led, to touch and explore the world

without sight. After ten minutes, immediately and quickly explore on the page. Where this has led you.

4) Creatures, Insects, Wild Animals. See how they can symbolize in a story or a poem. Write with the voice of a chosen creature.

5) Objects in a Bag. Seeing with your hands. Feel each one. Allow sharpened awareness to spill over into writing.

6) Autobiography. Write from the past. Focus on detail, particulars. Exactly how it was.

7) Images from Childhood. List of ten short sentences, each one a separate image. Discard three. Arrange the remaining seven in various sequences until you make the best poem possible.

8) Character. Describe a room so that it reflects the character of the person living in it. But without describing the person at all.

9) Character Sketch, He/She is... If he/she were a *sound*, what sound would he/she be? Reply with extended image, not just one word.

Repeat with: machine; part of the body; cloth; insect; a kind of light; piece of furniture; illness; ornament; food. Then devise your own.

10) The Wild Card. Collect unusual images on postcards. Pull one out at random and write at once from its impact on you. What does it call up in you? Respond, don't describe.

11) Dialogue Project. Work with a friend, write one line each of a poem, one paragraph each of a story.

12) Senses: Smell. Imagine entering a room which has an unknown, unrecognized smell. Track it down, feel it out in words.

Or a number of different smells. What do they suggest?

13) Dialogue Work: Extracts. Take a short extract from a poem. Ask questions of each other: what does this mean for you, remind you of, in *your* life? Write a poem *out of* the extract. This can be done alone.

14) Bending the Poem. Take the first verse of any poem of your choice. Discard the rest. Write a second verse, taking the theme in a new direction, as though the poem were hinged in the middle.

15) Take a Theme for a Walk. Time it, limited time is important. Keep the idea or image in front of your mind and see what springs up from the world to connect with that theme and to give to it.

16) Pudding-Bowl Poems. Good in workshops but you can adapt for your own use. Make a list of images on a piece of paper – fragments, lines of songs, your own previously written lines or new ones. Tear into separate strips, fold and mix in a bowl. If you put ten into the bowl each day, at the end of the week you'll have enough to surprise yourself. Pull out ten, make the best possible poem out of seven, discarding three.

17) Bring Objects Alive. Imagine you are object, plant. Write how you are, what you see. Complain! Are you locked in? Or liberated?

18) Way-stones. (Stations of the Cross.) Walking, carrying a notebook, decide to stop in 12 places. When you come to a place that feels good, potent, potential, stop and observe. Each time, jot down how it is there, what you see, feel, hear both inside and outside.

19) Photograph. Choose a photograph of yourself, or of someone close to you. Keep it by you for a few days. Write as though she/he is a stranger to you.

20) When I Am Old. Imagine you are old, eccentric, and you can have all the things you ever wanted, however impossible. Imagine it, either what you will do or have, or have just done.

21) Morning Focus. Each morning on waking, explore the first moments of consciousness. The territory of bed, your body. Getting up. How? Where are you going? What is with and within you, in this rising? Do this each day for one week. *Forms*: dialogue with yourself; first person reflection; third person narration, as though looking at yourself.

22) From the Mind of a Child. Event, action or person seen from the point of view of a child. Check sizes, language, distress, curiosity. Innocence. Cunning.

23) Cloth-scene. Tell the story of an event which is full of the feel, name, texture of cloth and clothing.

24) Dialogue Work. Choose an object, part of your body,

furniture. Speak to it. Create many moods. Have it speak back.

25) Frankenstein. Use various objects to describe him. His character, his walk. Don't worry about reality and *literal* truth. One way of doing this is to assemble objects in advance, in reality or in imagination, eg fire-tongs, saucepan, bucket. Thus: his hands are the glint of tongs as they shuttle the coal; his head is the rounded steel of a saucepan in which his thoughts cook, etc.

26) Sharpening Language. Write a prose-piece. Cut it by half, exactly, from the first word-count. Sharpen the language, say the same thing and *as much* in half the space.

27) Questions and Answers. Write ten questions, ten answers. Cut up, fold and put in Question Box and Answer Box. Take one from each and put together.

28) Unsent Letters I. Write to: DOCTOR; PRIEST; PROFESSOR; TEACHER; BOSS; MOTHER; FATHER; CURRENT PRIME MINSTER OR PRESIDENT.

29) Objects on a Tray. Memory-test with writing. Gather a tray full of objects. Look at them for five minutes. Put them away. Don't try and remember everything, but take what's remained in your mind, what stands out.

30) Unsent Letters II. Write a letter to your hand, foot, eye, nose, etc. Approach could be: reproachful; severe; playful; furious; appreciative; sarcastic; compassionate.

Be watchful always for where the accurate recording of things moves into invention. Do not resist the divergence between a copy of what's there and your inventions, exaggerations and extravagance. Do not resist the pressure of your imagination to shift, divert and interfere with it – either what you are writing about (how you see it) or the words you use (how you write it).

List C: Long-Range, Completions, Comprehensives

1) Themes. Use a theme to take you through a week. Complete a story or poem. Themes might be: HANDS; CAPTURING ANIMALS; THE THIRD WOMAN; FOOD; EARTH,

AIR, WATER, FIRE; WEEDS; LOOSE ENDS; HALF-WAY HOUSE.

2) Found Theme. Using the span of a week, do the same as in 1) but take a sentence at random from a book.

3) Collected Themes. Buying a notebook for the purpose, collect themes that feel powerful for you: single ideas; scraps from songs; lines overheard; graffiti; jokes.

4) Given Theme. Arrange with a friend to have him send you a theme in an envelope. Use it as a *command to write*, as though you have been given a quest. Refuse to be diverted...

5) Spaces. Rooms; streets; shells; cupboards; corridors; fields. Inhabitable space: of the body; hut; corners; the space of words.

6) Crow's-feet, Widow's Hump. All manner of misshapen things. How did it come to be so? What is its meaning?

7) Still Life. Create your own, eg seven beach stones, address each one. How its markings remind you. Or write from the conjunction and arrangement of objects. Keep them in place for several days or a week.

8) Opening Lines. Write 20 opening lines of poems or stories. Wait 24 hours. Pick one and continue. Use the list over several months.

9) Visual-Verbal Project, eg HANDS. Collect pictures, music, songs, make notes, watch out for – over several weeks. This is your magnet. Draw, sing, dance as well as write it.

10) Collage. Using magazines, newspapers, make a collage of words and images found in the papers and adding your own.

11) Research. Take a theme from contemporary life. Make a project and gather material. Write short poems, interspersed with pictures, photographs, headlines, notes. You can make posters from this.

12) Fruits and Vegetables. Write from the point of view of a fruit or vegetable which is about to be eaten.

13) Monsters. What, or who, most frightens you? Past or present. Dead or alive. Create a monster from that person. Like a cartoon, extract prime features, exaggerate.

14) Opposite Sex I. Write a poem or story as though you were of another sex. A known person or imagined character.

15) Opposite Sex II. Write about a member of the opposite sex, real or imagined. Ideal, most feared etc.

16) Word and Image. Choose a theme of few words only. Choose an image, a photograph or picture. Use the juxtaposition of the two triggers to create poem or story. Try this with images that blend and images that are disparate.

17) Animals. Write from the point of view of an animal. Use the animal to focus on what it means to be human.

18) Horoscopes. Write your own horoscope, your own future. But make it strange, bizarre, perhaps impossible.

19) Obituary. Write your own. How you would like your life summarized at the end of it. How you would like a picture of your life to be.

20) Wills. Write your own. Not leaving just material possessions, but also qualities, vices, parts of the body. Leave these as well as material possessions to, for example, institutions, nature, public figures.

21) Story Construction. Write on three separate pieces of paper: a) a character; b) a place; c) an object. Weave your story to include all three.

Repeat as often as you like. Keep a store and mix them.

22) Spaceman Letter. Imagine you are on the way to the moon in the first space-shuttle. Write to someone close to you, how it is.

23) Histories. Write the story of a teacup, shoe, book.

24) Reincarnation. If you were to be born again as something else, what would you choose to be? What would you look like? Feel like? What would the world look and feel like from your point of view?

25) Lift in a Lorry. A story in which someone gets a lift in a car or lorry late at night. Check: the state they're in; character of driver; connection between two. What happens? Try to introduce an unexpected twist near the end.

26) Writing to Music. Explore as many different forms, speeds and moods as you can.

27) Acrostic. A poem in which the first letters of each line spell a word or a name.

28) Three Rooms. Write 100 words on the room you write in

now. One hundred words on a room you were in as a child and where you felt happy and secure. One hundred words on your perfect room.

Thus through the Real, to the Past, to the Ideal.

29) Working from Paintings. Visit galleries and look at paintings or sculpture.

Seek out abstract or distorted shapes in paintings.

Imagine waking up as a shape you have found in a painting or sculpture. Draw your new shape. How would you move? How would you feel? How would you spend your day?

You could also do this from home, working from your postcard collection.

30) Character Sketch. Imagine a character who has one very pronounced feature. Write a poem or story in which that feature leads or is the cause of a whole sequence of actions and events. Perhaps decides the person's fate or destiny, eg Cyrano de Bergerac and his nose...

Try to carry out a piece of work to completion if working from this list.

2 SAMPLE WORKSHOP: HEGEL'S JUG

One of the most powerful aspects of the written word is its capacity to create movement, both within the individual and in the individual's relationship to the world and themselves. Writing can be a valuable tool, therefore, in the creation of movement when a person is, in one way or another, experiencing immobility – a sense of being 'stuck'.

This may be immobility in a strictly physical sense: an accident, the process of ageing, disease of the limbs – restriction of the external environment in one form or another. Or there may be psychological immobility caused by any one of numerous life crises: loss of a close relationship, sudden unemployment, homelessness. Or even something less identifiable, an inexplicable and even frightening sense of dread, alienation, a feeling of not belonging, a lack of will or motivation, a bleakness about life in general.

This unexplained and apparently causeless sense of paralysis may keep a person 'immobile' as effectively as if they had a disease of the limbs. We have all experienced this at some time during our lives, even if momentarily. We have perhaps dreamt of being unable to run, even though chased by a savage dog or dark force without shape or name. Often the effects of a strong dream or nightmare, where we have been impotent in the face of danger and unable to take action to bring ourselves to a place of safety, can linger throughout the following day and may well be our dream speaking to us of something in our lives as yet unidentified, which poses a threat and dislodges our well-being.

So let us start with the simplest and most obvious of assumptions: writing is a journey which all of us can embark upon even if we are unable to walk across the room, even if it feels perilous to set out on a journey in any other sense. For example, the journey towards a friend, stranger, one's boss or parent, or crossing the space within a relationship. The space between two people in the same room can be as vast as a continent.

And we can go further and say that the writing-journey will not – indeed *cannot* – be the same or be a 'copy' of any journey we have made in the physical world. For the simple reason that once you start playing with words, you are exercising a freedom that the physical world does not allow. The imagination is free to do what the immediate environment stubbornly refuses to do – that is, to move.

It is also important to remember that words also will refuse to be confined within the channels and cavities that we would have them fit. And that the word-journey will be of a different *nature* and far more contradictory than anything we can do in the 'real' world.

In their movement, words can connect together things that are not literally connected. Can create spaces, conjure up things we have forgotten, make riddles and even make a confusion or a mess. Perhaps we don't allow ourselves this luxury in our 'real' world.

We can think of the world of the page, whether scrap-paper, notebook, whatever, as being different in time and space from the time and space we normally inhabit. In that world (which we will make for ourselves) we can stretch or swim, pretend and invent, discover, rage and touch things we haven't seen before. In venturing outwards into the language-dimension, and in the creation of movement 'out-there' on the page, we create also internal movement and expansion. Thus the writer is drawn into investigation and meaning without willing himself forward word by word. This miracle can happen however entrenched the person's sense of the world as a dead and closed place.

Again I emphasize that this condition of experiencing everyday reality as mute and immobile may be a passing state of weariness. Like post-Christmas blues. Or it may be a deeper condition where, for example, the person has suffered severe deprivation in early life (physical or emotional) and has held on ever since to keep that pain at bay.

I frequently run workshops where a single object or image is used as a 'trigger' or starting-point. Let us imagine such a guided workshop where a dozen students are seated round a table in the centre of which is a china jug printed with blue cornflowers, a jug provided by myself.

The first reaction may well be to say: all right, it's just a jug – so what? The student may well manage a short piece *describing* the jug, its literal and immediate appearance. But what if I suggest that the jug may have individual associations for each person there? That if the jug is seen as relating to something else, which may or may not be present in the room, it ceases to be a passive object, closed on itself? Instead, it takes on a different quality, the movement of suggestion or association. I am directing the students into a movement of both the jug and their imagination, at the same time.

In this situation, where the jug is shifted in the imagination of the students from being a 'mere' object to becoming an object which is the start of an imaginative journey, we have all at once created an opening in the shared space around the table for an investigation with as yet unknown results. And each student's primary association will be different and lead to the dredging up of different memories and scenarios which in themselves may touch upon a variety of emotions. Thus the emotional landscape will be an individual and unique thing, as well as the location, time, atmosphere and so forth, of the memories called forth.

The associations may be fragments, or only half-seen. If I say, 'What is your most immediate association with that jug?' the response may be a person, but in the form of a mysterious presence. The student may not be able to remember who it is. Or it may be that the student is led to a fully-fledged memory, such as her mother washing her hair over a sink, and the unpleasant sensation of shampoo stinging her eyes. So that for her, the jug has a 'sting', and we have connected together two object-sensations which at first sight were hidden, or did not exist at all, for her or for us, at that table. So what we have done is to 'open up the moment' to a series of connections, relationships, shapes, memories, which moment had perhaps been mute and barren at the outset.

This 'opening up' can be a gentle and easy process, or can be harsh and abrasive, as intrusive and terrifying a vision as if a dead friend appeared before your eyes. It depends on each person's relationship to that which is summoned.

Or one student may say, 'It doesn't make me think of anything.' In which case my questioning may take on a more specific and directive quality.

But the general launch-stimulus will be in the form of a question such as, 'What does it remind you of?' or 'What does it look like?' or 'What is your most immediate association with this jug?' And I will include such asides as telling students not to worry how far away from the object their association-chain takes them. Nor to worry whether the various images and fragments which they wrote down connect together in an obvious way.

In this situation, we will be doing a number of things

simultaneously. It is virtually impossible to separate psychological movement and expansion for the writer and the creation of literature., We will be introducing meaning by our own activity where none existed before. We will be creating movement within ourselves and on the page which will inevitably lead to forgotten moments of potency, and we will also be undertaking the ground-work for the making of poems or stories. This last aspect of the activity will not be mentioned as an aim of the workshop, since the directive to write a poem rather than to explore what happens when we play around with a jug can cause blocks, fears and refusals, both conscious and unconscious.

By way of a jug there will be a charting of history and experience having some kind of crude existence or shape on the page which will be different from the head-on outpouring of feeling and recent memory that journal-writing implies. The jug-theme acts both as 'container' and 'magnet' for what is to be conjured and collected out of each person's individual storehouse; just like a jug in fact.

Not only has an objective world been created, with the page as 'other', but each person's inner landscape will have changed.

3 BREAKING THE LANGUAGE: BRIGHTON WORKSHOP

I was half-way through this book when invited to run a workshop for the Brighton Festival. I called my workshop a *Write for Life* workshop and not a Creative Writing workshop, wanting to introduce a new perspective on language-use than is evoked by such offerings as: how to write creatively; how to write poems and stories; what are the essential requirements to get into print. Since my investigation is one that goes *behind* and beneath such enterprises, I began with different and more fundamental questions: what am I doing, what are we doing when we write? What is language doing and what is it doing to us and to others when we write?

The students were all women (by chance, since the workshop was for all comers) and all were experiencing a sense of confinement, loss of power, strait-jacketing in their language-use to date: language as imprisonment, as impenetrable, unchosen, in the service of others, forced; language itself making oneself dumb so that there was a sense of not knowing any longer what it means to create or to *own* one's own language.

For some this was a staleness in the writing they were doing under their own volition. For others, the constraints of the writing they had to do in their work-situation were creating for them a sense of language-as-imprisonment across the board. As a reaction to this, some had begun non-linguistic activity such as painting or dance, but they had also come to this workshop in the hope of transformation to unlock the verbal language rather than turn elsewhere.

The women were either non-employed and seeking change, movement, expansion, or were looking for a *breaking-open* of language due to the imprisonment of their language-use in journalism, business reports, literary criticism, marketing, advertising, librarianship (cataloguing).

In the preliminary discussion and introductions, we came to an agreement on three issues:

- That language either *discloses* or *prevents*, and this may or may not be directly caused by circumstances.
- That clichés are essential for practical and functional issues where instant information is crucial. But that clichés are imprisonment if employed indiscriminately and beyond their functional use.
- That language can either dictate or discriminate.

I began the workshop by introducing a number of ideas.

1) That my investigations had led me into a chicken and egg situation. Writing was as much to do with changing and

loosening my mind as it was to do with the nature and quality of what I put down. That it doesn't matter where you start from, practice or idea, practice or perception. Each influences the other in a continuous to-and-fro movement.

2) That it is useful to find a *lens* or *filter* through which to channel your experience and your writing. Each of the 18 chapters in Part I of this book provides such a lens as a means of approach.

3) Work from Part I, 'A Basket of Currencies'.

    a) Who are you? Be attentive to your changes.

Also permit yourself to *become* something you haven't been, ie start with the writing. Make a sentence and *be there*. 'I am …', then locate.

What are you most afraid to be thought of as? Write it.

    b) 'When I use a word…it means just what I choose it to mean – neither more nor less.'

Is this possible? Can a word have a contained meaning in this way? Can it be so isolated, in a vacuum?

Write down the single name of a well-known object.

What is the context, what else at once comes to mind? The idea of interplay: you, and the language itself, variously directing proceedings.

    c) 'That's a great deal to make one word mean.'

Let's look at how much can be packed into one word.

Write down an object of use.

What is the emotional resonance of using that object? Is it a block or a barrier? What is it an alternative to? Is not that object *loaded*, a carrier for *meaning, history*? *Association*?

4) The writer as actor.

Take a simple action, eg 'I opened the door and entered the room.'

Continue with a further sentence using each of the following personae. You are:

    a) A THIEF

    b) A SNOOP OR SPY

    c) JEALOUS

    d) CAMERA (snapshot)

    e) A FOOL

    f) A JOKER

    g) A PRISONER (of idea, geography, emotion or illness)

From discussion and practice the following project emerged for a longer piece of work to try out at home:

Project: to show how your writing/language is influenced or determined by a particular *confinement*. That if we take a step back, we can escape from a *given* confinement and be in a position to choose a new one for ourselves.

Objects to work around: a picture or postcard.

Alternatives: choose *two* confinements or prisons.

Approach the card with first one, then the other.

At this stage of the two-hour workshop, we had time for only one further shared investigation. We took the word 'cup' and I asked each student to write down their associations, keeping in mind the ideas covered thus far: how the word refuses to remain as simply 'cup' and how impossible it is to imagine a cup without qualities and without a landscape blossoming around it.

Each mini-story branched in a different way. The single cup flew in all directions: a vehicle for more than liquid, an alternative, a break in time, a relationship.

> Containment, idea; what's inside it, liquid, decoration; cup, cut-short sound; Charlie drinks char from cup; cup chosen instead of mug; breast and bra-size; ritual performance, brittle; boredom, mood; shape, form – buttercup, breast, cupness; in his cups; how much? cup and mug; colour, cup of joy, my cup runneth over; cup-of-coffee, word attached to content; break, have a coffee, cup disappeared altogether; trophies, joke; no cups, no support.

Out of these 16 improvisations (I've written only the first step of each) the group rediscovered joy and surprise in how the world can be opened up in so many different ways from one single innocuous beginning. The cups multiplied and flickered in the room, conjuring locations, situations, scraps of lives that were themselves material for further discovery.

The essentials were *connection* and *significance*. To transform the 'merely there' into its fuller presence and its use as a tool for further discovery and creation.

4 LAURA'S WEEK I: THE INSPIRATION OF THE TREE

I asked Laura to try out a writing project, almost an act of meditation. To choose an object and return to it at a certain time each day for seven days, and write out of that moment's feeling. She chose a tree in the garden of a house two doors down, that backs on to our terrace: a particularly beautiful tree and an unusually large one for such small back gardens.

Here is Laura's writing:

28 June
As I sat in my window seat, low to the ground, curved like a foetus I saw and thought of the tree before me, through my frame. It arched in the gap, rising to the occasion and weeping reflections down its leaves like memories.

Leaves varied and changed minds as the wind and sun worked as a team curving and flipping light through and over the green plates. Still as light they can be, but today is different. The wind, the wind gushes their peace, surging them like a crowd of protestors or spectators, eyeing the ground and sky simultaneously. The top leaves wave like banners, declaring – I'm here and you're looking at me. The lower leaves look like they're battling for supremacy, reaching to the banners for sympathy, for position. The wind dies and the lift is lowered, the leaves fall to their joints, flopping like a wrist.

29 June
I held the tree tight with my little fists dotted up its back bark. I felt its grooves and read its life-span, long was my conclusion, long and fortune-telling. How many eyes have you held? You wave at me like a seducer stroking my face with your green fingers, holding my chin and framing my face in your shade.

Each leaf a face, a life, each drunk on the sun, tipsy as a greenfly dotting the plain. I'll tie up my thoughts in your branches, wrap each stalk to my spine, suspend myself upside down on your nectar, love you tree.

30 June

I'm smaller than the tree, its sun-sprayed branches, curling tongs of time, touching the next tone, over my head. If I dance with the tree through my window, I can feel its partner, chest exposed, knotted in, bosom trees.

I wish I could shake hands with its roots, ask them how deeply they go, where their strength comes from. I could idealize the tree and say from my eyes, request its permission to be witness. Silence awakens in me with the tree, flushes the brain, doubles the size.

1 July

The light clouds the leaf's joy as it darkens the veins of guilt. I feel the tree's struggle. Its battle heightens its worth as I love it and read it.

Its presence is exceptional, its wood a life-cycle, supporting the page. It provides a shift in my perception, a barrage of green sentences, lacing the sky. The gaps fill my stomach and whiten my gaze.

2 July

As I fell off the window-sill and flew to my tree, dipping close to the ground and up to its face, I thanked my lucky stars it was a dream and then the tree loved me and I knew I had its hand in mine and we'd live together, forever in reality, its leaves circling my head.

3 July

My hair is like your leaves, tree. You stare and stare at me like some animal curious of my size, shape, eyes. I reach you with the angle of my head. I'm nearer to you then you are to me. The lines on your face crumble into design and like an archaeologist I pamper your skin, pot you in my grasp.

4 July

Music wisps your leaves into fiddle on the bough. Vibrating the hairs on my neck, plaiting them into rope pulling me towards you. The diameter of your waist which I lock my hands round into unit, into dance. I'm the maypole with you, mirroring your smile. Tree, speak to me, tell me what you hear, touch? Do you feel me? My hands feel your bark, my grooves mediating your skin through mine. You could hurt me if you wanted to, fall on me, pierce my bosom between the cage in my chest, tug at my conscience as they chop you down, when I said yes. When I prune you with my heart, I tear my own veins that don't fly out like yours. I need to prune you for your future, don't you understand? It's love that cuts you, Bonsai boundaries, I'll not force on you, for you are established, adult. I'm younger than you, many inches, pounds short of you. Sometimes you're large in my head and you frighten me with your nature, pushing into my room. I've never dreamt about you, yet you're still oh so true in my garden, in my suntrap and there I shall find you when I return and there you'll find me when you're reborn.

The above is Laura's original, unedited.

5 LAURA'S WEEK II: HORSEMAN

Laura then worked for another week with a postcard chosen at random from my 'pack'. It is a photograph of a sculpture, *The First Horseman of the Apocalypse* by Malcolm Poynter (illustrated on p. 182). As with the tree, she approached the picture each day for seven days and wrote out of her encounter with the image.

26 July

He's telling her horse tales again. His head slurping towards her nose under her chin, eyes staring at her forehead, painting the words like grooves on an ever-turning record.

Your nostrils are too big, she said. His ears widen.

His penis shielded with crossed hands protecting him from her invisible hand, cupping the curve, allowing a beanshoot gap to follow.

27 July

It doesn't suit you, she said. I'm sorry, he said.

It'll have to be the end, she said. OK, he said.

Graphs of skin flake into continents, into islands of charred seas. Mottled moonscapes shape a human buttock and breast. The horsehead juts like a beheaded god, dark eyes of reason pooling the centre, the bridge.

His powerful lips lake the head, creating an orifice of words, a tunnel of sorrow at his bodyloss.

28 July

Her belly pushes his bottom ripe and her head rounds the sharpness of his ears. His neck mountains hang lower than his throat, easing the choke.

I'm going to have a foal, she told him. He was pleased, his head turned into father and smiled.

29 July

She's peeled all of his disguise and discarded the body. Left is the head which she loves. She's falling in love with it so much she's vanishing.

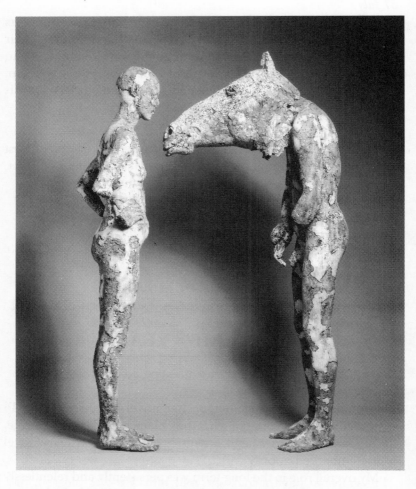

'The First Horseman of the Apocalypse' by Malcolm Poynter

30 July

He's taller than her, curved like a beanhair towards her bosom, shielding his heart from her glare.

31 July

Two trees of hidden flesh become a gate where the space supports their frame. Your eyes become fixed in their humility, their bareness. You poke imagination through the sieve reuniting it into a picture of ecstatic reality. Charred as they are, you love them, the hidden man, the bald woman. She's pregnant with his wildness, his imagination, bursting with wonder.

1 August

Legs, same height, pelvis tilt, arch of buttock, lean of trunk, burst of flower, eye of donkey, smoothness of skull, hills of breast, pump of hand, skin of lion, lips of God, dome of cathedral.

Pray to me, sweet horse, I love you.

The above is Laura's original, unedited.

6 MARIE'S YEAR

Marie and I worked together on her novel for three years. To write a complete account of what took place would be impossible. Or to reveal the content and structures of the extraordinary novel Marie embarked upon.

My overall role in the long-term was persistently and relentlessly to give Marie permission – to seduce, encourage and bully her into pushing her work to the extent of its possibility. If she was writing a bizarre scene, to carry it to the lengths of craziness.

When writing 'fully', we always think we're going over the top, not realizing that this is what writing is for – to break the mould, create what did not exist before, extend and stretch reality and ourselves from a latent potency into fully-fledged power. We are taught or persuaded (often covertly) to 'play safe', stay within the known, the given, to write a well-made and reassuring book which will deepen the reader's comfort and our own.

This 'giving of permission' and 'pushing further' are everpresent and underly all the various issues and problems that arise for students and which you'll recognize easily by now if you've read this far and not joined us right away at the Sample sections.

The following monthly chart covers the most pressing issues in either one or more hour-long tutorials in each month, for just over a year.

November
We covered the need for discipline, the excuse of no time, no space and so focused on the need for primary decision and resolution and its associative need, that of being able to say 'no' to alternatives in order to preserve writing time.

Recognition of the need to break up dense, direct speech and introduce tones and gestures to increase the sense of a living person talking and not just a disembodied voice.

Movement from: comfortable, bland, safe to fluid, provocative, mobile, resonant.

Recognition of 'ready-to-hand' words or phrases, ie the easiest, possible clichés. Develop capacity to *refuse* to use such and reach or search for the original phrase. Your own, previously unsaid. Using a word like 'charm', interrogate it. What kind, exactly? How is it manifested? Not simply 'He is charming' but 'His charm spread across the hotel reception desk like....'

December
Work on the word 'charm' to break it, stretch it. Discussion of need to focus on such grass-roots practice. This will then become an automatic turnover in the mind, part of one's mental/ imaginative apparatus.

The same scene built up from different angles. *Allow* the narrator (yourself) to have a number of viewpoints. Coming in to the same point/event from different directions.

Scattered, apparently loose ends build up a more coherent reality than one thinks when writing. In the reading, the time-spans shift. To say something in the most economical way or open it up into a fully-fledged reality. Introduce *lateral association* from object/scene itself – memory or expectation.

January

Tease out Marie's wonderful black humour that she doesn't quite trust. A tutorial hour of testing out how far it could go. Pressing for increase in eccentric quality. Resistance to 'being careful'.

February

Use of metaphor. Use of repetition. Reminder: *you* are the *author*. The crippling effects of comparison of self with other authors. In writing this, you are the *only* one. Worry about how the book takes its place in things later, ie keep a proper sense of an appropriate sequence of concerns. Write it down.

Recognition of Marie pausing to give full measure to all the sequence of moments.

March

Move out of story being worked on. Take time out for 'flexing muscles', forbidden if you insist on the preservation of sequence of actual text. The need for frequent movement away from formal work to preserve capacity for experiment, making a mess.

Keep several notebooks for parallel try-out work.

Make a *world* for yourself (to write in). Nobody cares. Nobody's watching.

Results in next session: pace, energy, attention to detail. Metaphorical vivacity. All fed back in from scribblings and diversions which have been tried out as separate projects. Note that some of these diversions will contain genesis of new work.

April

Question of the language needing to 'meet' and be adequate to the actual content. After five pages, the impact of actual events has worn off and the language is falling short. Explore devices for solving this: i) separate practice of choosing the most impossible and *in*appropriate adjectives/associations; ii) take on another persona to loosen grip of narrator as you are now; iii) blaspheme, break your own taboos; iv) leave story altogether and go for 'out of control' verbal improvisations.

When dealing with present-tense scene, power of introducing fragments of memory. Effect: to light it up, punctuate it, inject it with tension of something 'elsewhere' cutting through otherwise closed 'present'. (Idea of seamless, impenetrable present-moment.)

May

Need to pause in the writing and take stock. Suggest synopsis, as temporary (and expendable) *hold* to counteract sense of floundering. Discussion of need for balance between going-with-the-flow and firm framework. Give synopsis to me as need for objective summary, something held elsewhere.

Discussion and exploration of writing about sex. Recognition of how difficult this is. Ways forward.

Use of associative imagery to enhance sexuality. Use of unusual perspectives. Close-up/long-shot. Textures of things around. The flatness of straight clinical description.

At Laetitia Tronckh's house, a meeting of the TUFUC (Toss Up and Fuck Up Club):
Lui understood that penetration had not taken place. Peter, fearing broken ribs, clutched his arms across his chest and bunched his knees while executing a sideways roll. The huge bed contained his manoeuvre and held him. Connie, on the other hand, was catapulted up and over, feet first, revolved at speed through 180 degrees and returned to a sitting position astride Ramone's buttocks which billowed hospitably like an inflatable life-raft on the end of an overworked foot-pump. She had only had time to wrap a hank of Ramone's hair around her knuckles, preparatory to wrenching her neck until she forced her to quit the field, when Peggy and Candice took simultaneous racing dives on to the quilt. They set about scaling the barrage of her body and Ramone's to reach the satin lagoon where Peter floundered. Ramone was yelling that she couldn't breathe. Candice, a leg hooked around her neck, was tugging at Connie's left breast like the release cord on a parachute and had her mouth clamped on Peter's foot, under the impression that it was his penis. Peggy got mad and bit Candice in the ass while trying to pull *lui* over to her side with a noose she'd made out of Tronckh's pyjama cord.

June

We leave the novel to break across the potential paralysis of over-focus. Tackle reworking of story with ten-year-old narrator. Purpose: to keep the naive and trusting vision of a child. Create small incidents and gestures that 'flesh her out' in this way. Difference between *description* and *evocation*.

Advice: make sure she is always *in context.*

August

Return to the novel. Make an agreement to meet once a fortnight to create pressure and commitment, however aggravating!

Questions of expansion from within the text to extend and create fullness. Earmark various key moments within the flow of narrative as those which are more crucial than others. ie create graph of important/less important. Milk those for all you can get!

NB. Lateral association. Embroidery. }
NB. Refuse the easy route, push for 'more'. } reminders

Lui is Peter's penis with a mind of his own. Enlarge on his Machiavellian character. Suggest space-age technology imagery. Sentence structure echoing events.

The strident thrumming being emitted by the plants, or creatures, had grown much louder. It was, for Peter at least, an intimidating, almost unbearable sound. The denizens of the mushroom-field were intercommunicating with urgency and at high speed. When he had failed to mind his own business and just continue along the path he had taken, looking for shelter, he had thought the sound to be humming, but now he was sure it was talking. If a hundred thousand people gabbling on the phone – enquiring, assigning, gossiping, screeching, arguing, negotiating, pleading, pressing, promising, clinching, seducing and threatening, down the wires, could suddenly be made audible, without warning, to someone underneath taking a stroll – then this, he thought, was how it might sound. And what these smoothly bald and superciliously edible plants were saying had to have something to do with the precious, abundant, seemingly inexhaustible supply of seminal fluid which *lui* was hurriedly manufacturing to replace the fruits of its multiple orgasms, brought on by the intense and buoyant massage to which it was being subjected. Somehow or another the Field (Peter had ceased to think of them as individual mushrooms but rather as a unit of like-minded troops controlled by the central command at military headquarters in, and on, the Field) was capable of strategy. It was ensuring that it extracted the very last drop, not only of semen from the compliant and obliging *lui*, but also knowledge derived from its thorough reconnaissance of Peter's limbs, the pores of his skin, the interstices of his ears, the cavities of his nose, the irises of his eyes and, best of all, the strata of his brain. That is, if a brain like Peter's could be of any interest to anyone, even a mushroom, considering it had been dumb enough to get him into this situation in the first goddam place.

September

Check out alterations based on last time. Plus narrative position to increase sense of Connie *towering above him* in shower, narrative position located low down, as a camera-shot might be chosen for this effect.

Watch out for fall in energy. I call this watching 'raking the text'. Each time with different rake. When the text 'flags', find new starting-point *within* it and give it/yourself a kick-start. Permission to pretend you're starting again from that point, and so new energy.

Question: when the writer starts 'preaching', as though from outside.

Reconnect text to point-of-view of one of the characters. In this case, 'dare' lui's viewpoint?

October

Watch for cliché used positively or ironically – reference American writing and refer to 'Family' issue of *Granta*. Compare and discuss.

Again, raise question of 'rake-editing', one focus at a time. The question of *being there*, of *being* Laetitia Tronckh. Allowing this. Thus be prepared to extend yourself into other characters. Or find parts of yourself that empathize/identify with each. Problem of six bizarre and powerful female characters in one scene. Take time out and do a chart for each one. Play with the identities and differences and *then* feed into the master text.

November

NB *Granta*, the balance between the content and the manner of telling. Examine portraits of the six women at Mrs Tronckh's cocktail party. Careful long sentences. When each woman acts, *clue* to who she is:

1) Select a single bizarre or distinctive piece of clothing, eg hat veil knocking out a contact lens which falls under the heel.
2) Fighting to get the goodies, narrator briefly inside each consciousness, eg 'flash of Napilos de Derogation's head drowning under flying pizzas'.

NB. The present moment is *informed* by so much more than itself. Cut back or out to past and future and pull that in. Excellent mounting confusion, humour on bed. Approaching the bed-scene.

Out in the hall, broadcast back from the stairway, were the sounds of shrill accusations, the impact of well-upholstered bodies, moving at speed, in collision. There followed a squeal of outrage, hearty sobbing. Sandie, who more than made up for her lack of height by her pragmatic inventiveness, had removed half of the pair of sculpturesque white boots she wore and used the sharpened heel to prise up one of the stair-rods. It served as quite an efficient battering-ram with which to clear a path through the rear ends of the women who had preceded her into the passageway. She thought of her husband, Napilos – not for the first time – upended in a vat of pizza dough, his bough-legs waving ever more feebly as she poised the stair-rod above his buttocks. The vision had narrowed her saucer-eyes to lemon-segment apertures and she thrust the makeshift spear at random. It so happened that it connected with the base of the isosceles triangle that was, figuratively speaking, Ramone. Her lack of underwear certainly contributed to the intensity of pain produced by the point of the rod which easily pierced the unlined, spongy pile of her mud-brown frock, entering her flesh at the very confluence of the only-too-ample cheeks of her ass. Her ersatz leopardskin headgear lost the connection with its hatpin and descended into the maelstrom of running feet. Her lips parted and yellow ingots of teeth, interspersed with the ivory, sneered in a rictus of rage. Only pausing to pluck the weapon from her coccyx, she kept on running towards the upper rooms.

'The Extravagance of Being There' – how to create it. Narrative reflects/evokes what's happening. Language adequate to the scene, so that they meet.

How to proceed after a scene of such fever and verve?

December
How to change pitch and speed and still write vividly and strongly. Way in might be: what *sound* do you have in your head

for it? ie Marie always running ahead of herself, need to slow down now and see what's there. NB. Parts of a person are revealed, called up, invented to meet the demands of the work.

The writer as actor, discovering and inventing herself. Suggestions for next chapter: give Peter a dream? Write it in a number of ways?

a) completely externally; b) meander slowly; c) devise a number of concepts to enter 'in the mode of', eg Locomotion:- crawl, meander, stroll, flight; Location:- fly-on-the-wall, underfoot, hidden, ultra-mobile.

At the end of one year, a summary of what is now becoming second nature:

Various ways of raking through text to 'test' against desired result.
Multiple perspectives, metaphor, memory, lateral association.
Detail, the particular, the specific and precise 'thing'.
Starting again mid-stream as solution to energy-drop.
Re-organization of order/sequence.
Humour and imagery no longer generated only by sexuality but now coming into play in other areas.
Subterranean activity generated, so that it comes out as though natural.
New landscapes. Attention sentence lengths, pace, pitch.
Keep everything and everyone located, reference to detail, gestures to *focus* long descriptions/speeches.
The metaphor is a looped current, a circuit out and back.
Break novel down into smaller, manageable building-blocks.
Be prepared to be playful, subversive, vigilant to *own* avoidances. If you activate a scene in a certain way, you yourself will be activated as a result of your own invention. Writing does more than we think.
Fear of success.
Be prepared to deviate from main narrative.
Images in keeping with mood and sound level.
Necessary to launch ideas and yourself ahead of yourself and find out what it's about in further process.
Best writing comes from *mining* the area just held back and in potential.

Time-shifts in narrative. Attention overall frame.

Direct continuity not always necessary.

Multiple perspectives on same event.

Remember permission to move in and out of characters' thoughts.

Allowing yourself to go where you normally don't go.

Author's Note

I would like to express my gratitude to Marie-Rose Cluny, for our generative and subtle interactions, for permission to speak of what was exchanged, and to quote here extracts from her novel *The Peter Principle*.

FURTHER READING

Bachelard, Gaston, *The Poetics of Space*, Beacon Paperback, 1969

Berger, John, *And our faces, my heart, brief as photos*, Writers and Readers Publishing Cooperative, 1984

Berger, John, *A Fortunate Man*, Writers and Readers Publishing Cooperative, 1976

Berger, John, *Into Their Labours*, Granta, 1992

Berger, John, *Keeping a Rendezvous*, Granta, 1992

Berger, John, *Permanent Red*, Writers and Readers Publishing Cooperative, 1979

Bible, The, Authorized Version

Bly, Robert, *Iron John*, Element Books, 1990

Brown, Christy, *My Left Foot*, Secker and Warburg, 1954

Buber, Martin, *I and Thou*, T. & T. Clark, Edinburgh, 1970

Castaneda, Carlos, *Journey to Ixtlan*, The Bodley Head, 1973

Castaneda, Carlos, *The Teachings of Don Juan*, University of California Press, 1968

Carroll, Lewis, *Alice's Adventures in Wonderland*, Macmillan, 1952

Carroll, Lewis, *Through the Looking-Glass*, Macmillan, 1952

Dillard, Annie, *Teaching a Stone to Talk*, Pan Books, 1984

Dorfman, Ariel, *Death and the Maiden*: Afterword, Nick Hern, 1991

Feldenkrais, Moshe, *Awareness Through Movement*, Penguin Books, 1980

Field, Joanna, *A Life of One's Own*, Chatto & Windus, 1934; Virago Edition, 1986

Field, Joanna, *An Experiment in Leisure*, Chatto & Windus 1937; Virago Edition 1986

Heidegger, Martin, *Poetry, Language, Thought*, Harper & Row, 1971

Jackowska, Nicki, *The Islanders*, Harvester Press, 1987

Jackowska, Nicki, *News from the Brighton Front*, Sinclair-Stevenson, 1993

Jackowska, Nicki, *Voices from Arts for Labour*, Pluto Press, 1985

Kantaris, Sylvia, *Dirty Washing*, Bloodaxe Books Ltd, 1989

Merleau-Ponty, Maurice, *The Prose of the World*, Heinemann, 1974

Nicoll, Maurice, *Living Time*, Vincent Stuart Publishers, 1952

Ondaatje, Michael, *Coming Through Slaughter*, Picador, 1984

Ondaatje, Michael, *In the Skin of a Lion*, Picador, 1988

Osumi, Ikuko and Ritchie, Malcolm, *The Shamanic Healer*, Century Hutchinson, 1987

Rushdie, Salman, *Is Nothing Sacred?*, Granta, 1990

Sacks, Oliver, *Awakenings*, Penguin Books, 1976

Shakespeare, William, *Hamlet*, The New Clarendon Shakespeare, Oxford University Press, 1947

Stanislavski, Constantin, *An Actor Prepares*, Penguin Books, 1967

Steiner, George, *Proofs and Three Parables*, Faber and Faber, 1992

Steiner, George, *Real Presences*, Faber and Faber, 1989

Steiner, Rudolf, *Speech and Drama*, Anthroposophical Publishing Company, 1960

Steiner, Rudolf, *The True Nature of the Second Coming*, Rudolf Steiner Press, 1961

Tarkovsky, Andrey, *Sculpting in Time*, The Bodley Head, 1986

Teilhard de Chardin, Pierre, *On Love*, Collins, 1972

Wesker, Arnold, *Words as Definitions of Experience*, Writers and Readers Publishing Cooperative, 1976

Yeats, William Butler, *The Poems,* J. M. Dent & Sons Ltd, 1990
Zohar, Danah, *The Quantum Self,* Bloomsbury Publishing, 1990

The writings of C. G. Jung have informed my life and work, but have not influenced the creation of this book in any systematic way. More as a kind of 'presence'. For those readers who would like to explore more fully the ideas contained here concerning the nature of human beings, what is becoming lost in our culture, etc., I would say that Jung's thought will be helpful and perhaps come closest to how I see things.

USEFUL ADDRESSES

INTERNATIONAL

P.E.N. International
9/10 Charterhouse Buildings
Goswell Road
London EC1M 7AT
tel: 0171 253 4308

AUSTRALASIA

Australia Council
PO Box 788
Strawberry Hills
NSW 2012
Australia
tel: (02) 9950 9000

Australian Society of Authors
PO Box 1566
Strawberry Hills
NSW 2016
tel (02) 9318 0877

NORTH AMERICA

American Society of Composers,
   Authors and Publishers
One Lincoln Plaza
New York
NY 10023
tel: 212 621 6000

The Authors League of America, Inc
330 West 42nd Street
New York
NY 10036
tel: 212 564 8350

Canada, The Writers' Union of
24 Ryerson Avenue
Toronto
Ontario M5T 2P3
tel: 416 703 8982

Canadian Poets, League of
54 Wolseley Street
3rd Floor
Toronto
Ontario M5T 1A5
tel: 416 504 1657

SOUTHERN AFRICA

South African Writers' Circle
PO Box 10558
Marine Parade
Durban 4056
South Africa
tel: (031) 307 5668

UK and EIRE

The Arvon Foundation
Totleigh Barton
Sheepwash
Beaworthy
Devon EX21 5NS
tel: 01409 231338

The Arvon Foundation
Lumb Bank
Heptonstall
Hebden Bridge
West Yorkshire HX7 6DF
tel: 01422 843714

The Arvon Foundation
Moniack Mhor
Kiltarlity
Beauly
Inverness-shire IV4 7HT
tel: 01463 741675

Authors' Guild of Ireland Ltd
282 Swords Road
Dublin 9
(01) 375974

Authors, The Society of
84 Drayton Gardens
London SW10 9SB
tel: 0171 373 6642

Denehurst Writers' Centre
Alford Road
Mablethorpe
Lincs LN12 1PX

Federation of Worker Writers
    and Community Publishers
68 Grand Parade
Brighton BN2 2YJ

Fen Farm Writing Courses
10 Angel Hill
Bury St Edmunds
Suffolk
IP33 1UZ
tel: 01379 898741

Irish Writers' Union
Irish Writers' Centre
19 Parnell Square
Dublin 1
tel: (01) 8721302

Loch Ryan Writers
Loch Ryan Hotel
119 Sidbury
Worcester WR5 2DH
tel: 01905 351143

London Playwrights
80 Lordsmead Road
London N1 6EY
tel: 0181 808 7622

National Poetry Foundation
27 Mill Road
Fareham
Hampshire PO16 0TH
tel: 01329 822218

Playwright's Trust, New
Interchange Studios
Dalby Street
London NW5 3NQ
tel: 0171 284 2818

The Poetry Book Society
Book House
45 East Hill
London SW18 2QZ
tel: 0181 870 8403

Poetry Ireland
The Austin Clarke Library
Upper Yard
Dublin Castle
Dublin 2
Eire
tel: (01) 6714632

The Poetry Society
22 Betterton Street
London WC2H 9BU
tel: 0171 240 4810

Scottish Book Centre
137 Dundee Street
Edinburgh EH11 1BG
tel: 0131 229 3663

Welsh Union of Writers
13 Richmond Road
Roath
Cardiff CF2 3AQ
tel: 01222 490303

Writers' Guild of Great Britain
430 Edgware Road
London W2 1EH
tel: 0171 723 8074